"John Baldoni shows his exceptional understanding of taking highly complex components and simplifying them. _Grace Under Pressure_ analyzes great skills, which I think anybody who wants to become better at what they are doing should read. I would definitely recommend this book!" —**Martin Lindstrom**, _New York Times_ bestselling author of _Brand-Washed, Small Data_, and _Buyology_

"John Baldoni once again offers us powerful lessons in leadership and life. His new book _Grace Under Pressure_ will help you brace for the unexpected and hold it together when everything is coming apart at the seams. As you put these principles into practice, you'll find you and your team can be at your best when circumstances are at their very worst." —**Liz Wiseman**, _New York Times_ bestselling author of _Multipliers_ and _Impact Players_

"In times of change, people look for a leader with the strength and resilience to persevere and the ability to lead with empathy and conviction. _Grace Under Pressure_ by John Baldoni shows how leaders put people first, take care of themselves, and prepare for what's next. This book is for executives looking to steady themselves and their teams for change and crisis." —**Marshall Goldsmith**, the world's pre-eminent executive coach and _New York Times_ bestselling author of _The Earned Life, Triggers,_ and _What Got You Here Won't Get You There_

"John Baldoni has done the world a favor by introducing the language of grace into our conversation about leadership. I was a huge fan of his wonderful book *Grace*, and *Grace Under Pressure* continues this tradition, showing why grace is most effective in times of maximum pressure. The ability to exhibit courage and calm in our most challenging moments is precisely what inspires others to trust us, giving them the confidence to stay engaged when the going gets rough. *Grace Under Pressure* is not only inspiring, it is practical. Throughout the book, John offers questions for our consideration to identify how and where grace might be operating in our own lives so we can let it influence our relationships and actions." —**Sally Helgesen**, bestselling author of *How Women Rise, Rising Together, The Web of Inclusion*

"*Grace Under Pressure* reveals what leaders must do to look ahead past the crisis the same time they are caring for their teams. It's powerful preparation for every leader's inevitable tough times." —**David Novak**, former CEO of Yum! Brands, podcast host of How Leaders Lead, and author of *New York Times* bestseller *Taking People with You* and *Take Charge of You*

"If you can feel the screws tightening…this might be the book you need to find your grace under pressure." —**Michael Bungay** Stanier, bestselling author of *The Coaching Habit* and *How to Begin*

"Leadership is never easy, but when there's great change or crisis, the heat is on. Fortunately, John Baldoni has provided leaders with a practical, powerful, and wise guidebook: *Grace Under Pressure*. This will be an essential tool for leaders under stress." —**Dorie Clark**, *Wall Street Journal* bestselling author of *The Long Game* and executive education faculty, Duke University Fuqua School of Business

"Leadership is revealed in times of crisis. *Grace Under Pressure* by John Baldoni provides insights into how to make your leadership resonate with purpose and grace. Leaders must care for their teams and themselves as they prepare for the future. Even better, they must do it with grace—caring, commitment, and courage." —**Garry Ridge**, the Culture Coach and Chairman Emeritus of the WD-40 Company

"With the spotlight shined on modern-day business leaders, there's a greater demand to do more than be savvy and apply business acumen. Today's leaders are expected to care and act out of concern not just for the company and its employees but to grasp how their role affects the greater welfare of all. *Grace Under Pressure* by John Baldoni shows us how to lead with courage, conviction, and compassion, especially in times of stress and urgency." —**Donald Altman**, author of T*he Mindfulness Toolbox, Simply Mindful,* and *Clearing Emotional Clutter*

"John Baldoni's new book is a beautiful example of combining science, practice, real-life examples, and deep humanity to offer ways for a modern leader to lead. I particularly like John's combining 'taking care of self' with the aspects of taking care of people and preparing for the future. The Considerations that anchor each chapter are great coaching questions and wonderful ones to ponder and resolve. *Grace Under Pressure* is an easy read and yet leaves you with great reflections and practical tools to move forward." —**Magdalena Nowicka Mook**, CEO, International Coaching Federation (ICF)

GRACE

LEADING THROUGH

UNDER

CHANGE AND CRISIS

PRESSURE

GRACE

LEADING THROUGH

UNDER

CHANGE AND CRISIS

PRESSURE

JOHN BALDONI

SAVIO
REPVBLIC

A SAVIO REPUBLIC BOOK
An Imprint of Post Hill Press
ISBN: 978-1-63758-756-0
ISBN (eBook): 978-1-63758-757-7

posthillpress.com
New York • Nashville
Published in the United States of America

1 2 3 4 5 6 7 8 9 10

Also by John Baldoni

Grace Notes: Leading in an Upside-Down World (2021)

Grace: A Leader's Guide to a Better Us (2019)

Moxie: The Secret to Bold and Gutsy Leadership (2015)

The Leader's Guide to Speaking with Presence: How to Project Confidence, Conviction, and Authority (2013)

The Leader's Pocket Guide: Indispensable Tools, Tips, and Techniques for Any Situation (2012)

Lead with Purpose: Giving Your Organization a Reason to Believe in Itself (2011)

The AMA Handbook of Leadership (2010), edited by Marshall Goldsmith, John Baldoni and Sarah McArthur

12 Steps to Power Presence: How to Assert Your Authority to Lead (2010)

Lead Your Boss: The Subtle Art of Managing Up (2009)

Lead by Example: 50 Ways Great Leaders Inspire Results (2008)

How Great Leaders Get Great Results (2005)

Great Motivation Secrets of Great Leaders (2004)

Great Communication Secrets of Great Leaders (2003)

180 Ways to Walk the Motivation Talk (2002), co-authored with Eric L. Harvey

Personal Leadership: Taking Control of Your Work Life (2001)

180 Ways to Walk the Leadership Talk (2000)

To my grandsons,
Tripp and Giovanni.
May the future be yours

Contents

Part 3: Prepare for the Future

Part 4: How to Lead with Grace Under Pressure

Prologue:
Grace Under Pressure

Grace Under Pressure.

When I hear that phrase, what comes to mind is the five-alarm fire. There's a lot of heat and there's a lot of noise and a lot of people scrambling around.

But if you look closely between the fire trucks, you'll see a battalion chief on site, calmly giving directions…with a very composed and collected demeanor.

That's what Grace Under Pressure is.

Grace Under Pressure means meeting…

> *Anger with composure.*
> *Denigration with respect.*
> *Sadness with compassion.*
> *Scarcity with abundance.*
> *Insults with smiles.*
> *Selfishness with selflessness.*
> *Hoarding with generosity.*
> *Life with gratitude.*

Today everyone is looking for a leader who can exhibit Grace Under Pressure.

Be collected. Be calm. Be composed.

This is someone that others can look to as trustworthy.

COPING WITH CHANGE

Change is the medium of our lives. Few things remain the same. What we know as reality may be gone tomorrow.

We learned this story during the pandemic. Suddenly the personal security many felt was consumed by the fear of becoming infected with a virus that could be as mild as nothing or as deadly as organ failure.

Fear of contagion provoked an economic crisis that closed businesses, many for good. It forced other people into unsafe work environments. And, it stretched our healthcare system to the breaking point.

Looking back, now that we can catch our breath, we know we can never again be complacent. Leaders will always face challenges, and how they conduct themselves when the pressure is on will be remembered for a long while.

When John F. Kennedy, then a US Senator, was finalizing his 1956 book, *Profiles in Courage*, he wanted to use the phrase, "grace under pressure." Kennedy's editor, Evan Thomas of Harper & Brothers, discovered that novelist Ernest Hemingway had used that phrase in a 1929 interview he gave to one of the leading contemporary observers of her time, the author and satirist Dorothy Parker, for an interview that appeared in the *New Yorker* magazine. It was a phrase in reference to courage that suited both the novelist as well as the future president; both were able to function in extremis, when tensions were high.[1]

"Grace Under Pressure" describes what it takes to remain calm in moments of urgency, when things are coming apart at the seams. Fight or flight takes hold. Many do the latter; leaders must select the former. Their future, as well as the futures of everyone around them, lies in the balance.

Good leaders do three things:

One, they take care of their people, putting their needs first so they can ensure the organization survives.

Two, they take care of themselves, making certain to be at their best because that's what is demanded of them.

Three, they prepare for the future, thinking and doing what it takes to engage others to build a better tomorrow.

It is not enough to do one or two; it is imperative to do all three, often simultaneously.

BUILD COMMUNITY

As important as these three steps are, there is something more—grace. In previous writings, I have defined grace as the catalyst for the greater good.[2] That definition still holds for me. When it comes to dealing with change and crisis, grace becomes evident in how we treat one another. Grace facilitates our ability to connect with ourselves more genuinely so that we can connect more humanly with others. Such connections are essential to keep oneself together when everything around seems to be falling apart. These connections do something even better: they create community, a place where people want to be because they feel they belong.

Grace Under Pressure: Leading through Change and Crisis will provide insights into how to achieve leadership through both change and crisis, and how to do it well. Augmenting the stories are interview comments from thought leaders in business and human development about how to overcome feelings of uncertainty, anxiety, and stress. Resilience is essential. Learning to adapt to changing situations and to bring others along with you is essential to survival.

Grace Under Pressure: Leading through Change and Crisis is a look at how leaders focus on what's in front of them as well as what they need to do to prepare for a better tomorrow.

> *When the heat is on, good leaders step forward.*
> *They demonstrate that they have what it takes to deal with the pressure…and they bring others along with them.*
> *Grace Under Pressure.*
> *It's a good thought for our times.*[3]

Part 1

TAKE CARE OF YOUR PEOPLE

© 2020 Ted Goff

"When I asked for ideas about how I could be a better boss, I didn't want so many."

Leaders prove their mettle when times are toughest.
Face adversity with steely eyes and square jaws.
Alleviate stress among others by lessening the load.
Bend but do not break and teach others how to do the same.
Empathize to make things better.
Inspire by citing the examples of others.
Affirm the values of individuals, teams, and the organization.
Show they care by acting with care, compassion, and commitment.
Create community where people feel they belong.

Put Your Values into Action

Caring for your people begins with a commitment to values. Values are the bedrock of any organization. It isn't easy to maintain our bearings with everything breaking and shaking around us, but so often we see that when an organization survives tough times, it is their values, their collective beliefs, that hold them together.

We cannot control events or circumstances, but we can control how we react to them and how we move forward through them. With that in mind, here are the values that I believe we need now more than ever.

Integrity. With upheavals come confusion and sometimes chaos. It can be hard to discern what's real and what's not. That is why it is imperative (double underscored) that leaders hold a torch on what's right and what's not. Leaders must reflect our moral compass.

Truth. The discernment of the way forward is rooted in the truth. Again, when everything is askew, it can be easy to favor the quick over the steady, the easy over the hard, and the hard over the soft. The arbiter of what must be done is truth. Without truth, there is only muddle.

Humility. The future is unknown. The "new normal" may not be entirely new or entirely familiar, but it will be what it will be. Humility is a reflection of vulnerability; it is the self giving itself permission to say, "I don't know everything." A leader who admits that is a leader who draws people toward them.

Reason. The ability to hold oppositional thoughts in mind is critical thinking. A leader must weigh the options using reason to discern truth and make decisions anchored in logic but rooted in love.

Courage. What is courage but an expression of bravery? A willingness to stand defiantly in service of a greater good over venality and mendacity? A courageous individual sets an example for others to be or to achieve something better.

Humor. Is humor a value? Well, if it's not, it should be, because only by looking on the wry side of life will we be able to deal with the darkness and dread that encroaches. The release of humor is laughter, and it is laughter that affirms that we are alive. Why? Because we can look at all that's around us and find lightness. Laughter is a release mechanism. Like letting air out of a balloon, laughter shakes our tensions and thereby relaxes us.

Grace. Grace is a gift without strings that we pass along to others. In doing so, we help others, and in turn, we help ourselves. Grace is the ability to give generously, to forgive readily, to show mercy, and to love without conditions. Grace lubricates living.

Lest this reflection turn into a sermon, let me add that these virtues must be coupled with the business drivers that will enable us to put our people back to work cooperatively and collaboratively. Such drivers include acumen, accuracy, and agility, as well as accountability and responsibility.

The emperor-philosopher Marcus Aurelius could have been reflecting on times like ours when he wrote, "Think of yourself as dead. You have lived your life. Now take what's left and live it properly. What doesn't transmit light creates its own darkness." Good words for all of us. We ponder what to leave behind and what to take with us on our journey forward.

By no means is this list of values comprehensive. Feel free to add your own. Please do, because it means you are thinking of what you hold dear so that you will be certain to take it with you as you shape your new normal for your team, your family, and yourself.

CONSIDERATIONS:

- How am I using my values to move ahead?
- Of the values listed above, which are most important to me? Why?
- What value would I add to this list?

Turn Your Organization into a Community

Values are the by-product of purpose—our why. Purpose sparks our vision—our becoming. It develops our mission—our doing. Purpose catalyzes us to achieve, but it does not say *how* we can achieve. Many people achieve greatness by acting more as a bulldozer than a tractor. A bulldozer flattens. A tractor pulls. In the former, the bulldozer steamrolls obstacles, even people. In the latter, a tractor drives ahead, drawing others in its wake.

There is a way to make purpose more compelling and appealing. We call it grace, a catalyst for the greater good.

Purpose is not inherently full of grace. Instead, it is powered by ambition, drive, and ego. Those are positives when they are used by a true leader, one more interested in bringing people together than in steamrolling opposition.

HOW GRACE TRANSFORMS PURPOSE

Grace complements purpose. If purpose is our why, then grace becomes our how—the way we do things here. Grace shapes the values that bind members to one another. Values underscore people feeling wanted. They believe they have a stake in the outcome. They know they belong. Grace transforms an organization into a community.

Grace is inherent to the human condition. Some might say our DNA includes it because we, as humans, true to our tribal nature, are inclined to help those closest to us. Grace, however, knows no biological kinship; it creates spiritual kinship. We are connected to others.

THINK ABOUT MUTUAL BENEFIT

An organization without grace is one where people feel fearful, uncertain, and perhaps unloved. Without grace, there can be no community. There may be an organization, but there is no connection. People feel they do not belong.

My colleague Mark Goulston, M.D., a business psychiatrist and bestselling author, often talks about the need for people, especially those at risk for self-harm, to "feel felt." Organizations can be alienating. Communities are embracing. In short, people feel emotionally connected to others within community. In the words of Dr. Goulston, they "feel felt."[4]

An organization with grace becomes a community. A community shares ideas, collaborates more closely, and endures hardships. It knows sacrifice for the greater good. It is rooted in purpose. Its members understand what the organization wants to achieve and they are committed to working toward the vision, accomplishing the mission, and embodying the values they espouse.

Organizations are administrative. They are formed to do something. They are artificial constructs. At the same time, because they are human creations, they can be made better.

They can become communities where people feel they belong and can contribute to something greater than themselves.

ENABLING GRACE

Grace facilitates our connections to one another. Grace complements psychological safety, a concept that author and professor Amy C. Edmondson of Harvard Business School has developed. When people feel safe, they can speak their minds, share their thoughts, and work cooperatively and collectively. Psychological safety encourages collaboration.

With grace, we do the following:

- Put others first.
- Listen before speaking.
- Look for problems to solve.
- Encourage people to speak out.
- Instill hope in the face of adversity.
- Drive out fear.
- Act with courage.

Doing so enables us to integrate purpose into our lives and create community with others.

CONSIDERATIONS:

- Here's a thought experiment: consider your place of work. Do individuals feel as if they belong to a community?
- If so, how do people express this sense of belonging?
- If not, what can you to create a community?

Learn from Adversity

When adversity strikes, people look for direction and guidance. That's why leaders must invoke purpose to provide a way forward.

"Adversity does not build character; it reveals it."[5] It will be the revelation of character that is necessary. Employees are looking to leaders who do not shirk from responsibility, but rather embrace the challenge. Such leaders do not hold themselves apart; they bring along others with them. They delegate responsibility and authority, all while remaining in the loop to monitor what is happening.

As bad as any crisis is—such as the pandemic—it will present us with opportunities. What those opportunities are may be unknown, but as the saying goes, "Never let a good crisis go to waste." Leaders must be thinking ahead as soon as they are able.

Accordingly, adversity reveals more than character; it also shines a light on talent. Women and men who have gone unnoticed suddenly find themselves in the spotlight with an opportunity to apply their skills to emerging problems. Doing so will mark them as people to give more responsibility and eventual promotions.

While we all hope that this crisis will pass in short order, health experts warn that more novel viruses will plague us in the future. How leaders act today will set the tone and pattern for how we deal with future crises.

William Goldman wrote the novel and screenplay for *The Princess Bride*. Called a fairy tale for adults (as well as children), the story involves love both unrequited and requited. It contains much hilarity as well as some words of wisdom, especially now. "Life isn't fair, it's just fairer than death, that's all."[6]

True enough for our times. Life as we know it has changed, but as every leader realizes, it sure beats the alternative.

> *Troubles have a way of shrinking some,*
> *But elevating the minds and hearts of others.*
> *Follow me, they say. I will lead.*
> *Come along, they say.*
> *Together we will make our way.*

CONSIDERATIONS:

- Think of a time you felt overwhelmed by a challenge.
- How did you deal with the challenge?
- What would you do differently now?

Build Resilience into Your Organization

Never is the need for clarity more urgent than during a time of crisis. Few of us like working in ambiguity. That's where organizational resilience enters. Such resilience facilitates a sense of community.

Every employee wants clarity and certainty in their jobs. One thing we teach managers is to set clear expectations and communicate them directly. Such thoughts are the basic principles of management.

Gareth Tennant, a member of the Future Strategy Club, says that organizational resilience relies upon planning for the unexpected and gaming the outcomes. For Tennant, a one-time Royal Marine (now a reservist), such practices are not wholly theoretical. Royal Marines, akin to US Special Forces, are assigned specialized jobs involving maintaining security in hostile territory. Tennant, whom I first encountered in the workplace column of the *Economist*, tells the story of an encounter with Somali pirates which occurred off the coast of Yemen in 2010.[7]

The Somalis were disarmed before entering the skiff but sought to overwhelm the three Marines in a moment of panic. The situation turned from calm to bedlam in less than a minute. As Tennant explained to me, his Marines had prepared for such a moment. "We talked through how things might change, what scenarios we might find ourselves in…from having to go lethal and having casualties…all of these different scenarios." So what could have been a disaster with casualties resolved itself with the quick thinking of one of the Marines who fired a warning shot into the water.[8]

Tennant explained that while that exact scenario had not been rehearsed when the unexpected happened, the Marines reverted to their training and dealt with the situation quickly and safely without casualties. That is a form of organizational resilience.

APPLYING LESSONS IN CIVILIAN LIFE

Today, in his civilian role as a strategist, Tennant helps companies deal with the unexpected. Again, while few companies could have foreseen the impact of a pandemic, those organizations that did respond positively were able to because they had a culture that included preparing themselves for the unexpected.

Stress testing assumptions through a process known as "red teaming," a technique borrowed from the military, enables a company to evaluate its strategic intentions by subjecting them to several different variables, such as market forces, competitors, or economic changes.[9]

Tennant embraces the concept of "divergent thinking." As he says, "It's not predicting the future." Divergent thinking is a process that enables a team to "respond to a range of future scenarios, allowing and empowering people to then adapt those response plans as they find themselves confronted with the reality."[10]

A LEADER'S RESILIENCE

Organizational resilience rests on the ability of a leader to be resilient themselves. Their resilience may come from their life story but also from how they perform in times of crisis. How they conduct themselves when the pressure is on sets the example for how their team responds. When the leader maintains composure, the group maintains order. Conversely, when the leader flails, team cohesion frays.

Essential, too, is a sense of humility. "A key attribute of leadership," says Tennant, is "being humble enough to accept that you don't have all the answers all the time, and you can turn to your team and get those answers." You must be "humble enough to try things and accept that you're gonna [sic] make mistakes. It's how not only as individuals, but as teams, we learn."[11]

In times of adversity, no one has all the answers. You need the entire team to coalesce. A leader who is willing to embrace alternative views, especially those not his own, is one who can engage hearts and minds to pursue new courses of action.

Clarity in the face of ambiguity may be elusive, but leadership in the face of adversity helps provide the resilience an organization needs to survive.

CONSIDERATIONS:

- How will I teach myself to think beyond the borders, e.g., scenario planning for never-never land?

- How can I teach my people to engage in "divergent thinking?"
- How will I make humility a necessary virtue for preparing for the unexpected?

Make Resilience Integral to Leadership

A modern airliner has upwards of two million parts. The reason for the considerable number is redundancy. There needs to be a backup component or system that can be activated automatically in case of an emergency. When you are flying at 30,000 feet and more than 560 miles an hour, redundancy is a must-have.

In times of crisis, organizations need redundancy, and so do their leaders. Redundancy is an insurance policy for resiliency.

Resilient leaders manage with redundancy in mind. First off, they make certain that someone can step into their role should they leave unexpectedly. Secondly, they prepare their organizations. "Organizations that deploy a 'good jobs' strategy have policies around cross-training and developing people so that if one unit or group falls short, others in the firm can pitch in because they have been pre-trained to do those jobs," says Rita Gunther McGrath, author of *Seeing Around Corners* and professor at Columbia Business School. "If staff only know how to do one thing, in a crisis, they are only useful with respect to that one thing, and if that's not the critical bottleneck, there is a real wasted resource."[12]

DEVELOPING RESILIENCE

A way to build redundancy within individuals is through self-discipline, willfully shutting out distractions so you can focus more acutely. "Intentionality probably builds some slack into our responses, because we're not using up a lot of bandwidth by diffusing our focus," says Sally Helgesen, a prominent authority on women's leadership and co-author with Marshall Goldsmith of *How Women Rise*. "So, if something unexpected occurs, we will have more mental resources—as well as physical energy—to respond quickly and effectively. And that definitely enables us to be resilient."[13]

Resiliency often begins with a whack, a metaphorical smack that levels you because it is often unexpected. There is no shame in being knocked down. It is what you do next that matters. There is a Japanese saying: "Fall down seven times, get up eight."

Warren Bennis, the noted leadership author and university president, posited the "crucible of leadership," a sort of trial-by-fire experience. Bennis's personal leadership crucible began as a nineteen-year-old lieutenant replacement during the Battle of the Bulge. Knowing no one, Bennis led his troops by relying upon his first sergeant. [14,15]

Resiliency is nurtured through a deep sense of self-awareness. Harry Kraemer, former CEO of Baxter, Inc and professor of leadership at Northwestern's Kellogg School of Management, advises being kind to yourself. "You're going to do the right thing, and you're going to do the best you can do." Kraemer recommends using this mantra when the worst happens. "I try to repeat this over and over again. Worry, fear, anxiety, pressure, and stress can be significantly reduced."[16]

SELF-AWARENESS

Just as airliners have redundant systems, so too can leaders. Individual redundancy depends upon self-awareness—knowing your strengths and weaknesses. During a crisis, your weaknesses may be exposed, so you need your personal backup system. For example, if you are a big-picture strategist, you will need detail-oriented people to help plot recovery tactics.

Furthermore, stress means we may over rely on what we do well. Such compensation creates overuse, and eventually, you will drive good people away. That is, an overly confident and assertive leader will fall into the trap of exerting himself into all problems, thereby undercutting the people tasked with finding solutions.

Sally Helgesen, a colleague of mine, believes that we can build resiliency by limiting the time we spend multi-tasking. "When we ask our minds to focus on two things at once, our bodies perceive that as stress." While you cannot eliminate stress, you can lessen its impact by focusing deliberately on the issue at hand before moving to another issue. "This is why being intentional, deliberate and mindful," says Helgesen, "is key to resilience."[17]

Times of crisis require an executive with personal and organizational redundancy that enables resiliency in the face of adversity. Such resilience builds connections that reinforce a sense of community.

CONSIDERATIONS:

- What experiences have made you more resilient?
- How can you demonstrate resilience to your team?

How Leaders Inspire during a Crisis

You have to be able to inspire!

We look to our leaders for inspiration.

Always in times of trouble, we look to those in authority to provide direction.

The challenge for leaders in such times is to project a sense of self-control in the face of the uncontrollable and calmness in the face of anger and rage. Here are some examples of leaders doing it correctly.

One example of a leader who exemplified what it takes to inspire others in a time of crisis is President Volodymyr Zelensky of Ukraine. Vladimir Putin had been threatening to invade Ukraine since Russia took over Crimea in 2014. Zelensky, a former comedian and actor, was elected president in 2018 after his predecessor, essentially a puppet of Russia, was overthrown. The shadow of Russian aggression hung over his leadership, but he did not flinch.

President Zelensky, whose most famous acting role was that of a schoolteacher who becomes president, has risen to Churchillian heights. Throughout the invasion, he has remained in Kyiv and spoken to his fellow citizens daily. And like Winston Churchill, he has appealed to the outside world for help and enlisted their aid in defense of his nation.

WHAT PRESIDENT ZELENSKY SAID TO CONGRESS

On March 16, 2022, President Zelensky addressed the joint houses of Congress via video conference. He was in Kyiv, which was under attack, and Congress was in Washington. (His remarks were given through a translator.)[18]

Creating context

Right now, the destiny of our country is being decided. The destiny of our people, whether Ukrainians will be free, whether they will be able to preserve their democracy. Russia has attacked not just us, not just our land, our cities. It went on a brutal offensive against our values. Basic human values. Against our freedom, our right to live freely, choosing our own future. Against our desire for happiness, against our national dreams.

Embracing the American context

Remember Pearl Harbor. The morning of December 7, 1941, when your sky was black from the planes attacking you. Remember. Remember September 11. A terrible day in 2001 when people tried to turn your cities into battlefields. When innocent people were attacked from the air. No one expected it. You couldn't stop it.

Stating the problem

> *Our country experiences the same every day. Right now, this moment, every night for three weeks, in various Ukrainian cities, Russia has turned the Ukrainian sky into a source of death for thousands of people. Russian troops have fired 1000 missiles at Ukraine. They use drones to kill us with precision.*

Call to action

> *For every person who works diligently, who lives honestly, who respects the law, we in Ukraine want the same for our people. All that is a normal part of your own life. Ladies and gentlemen, Americans, in your great history you would understand Ukrainians. Understand us now. We need you right now…If this is too much to ask, we offer an alternative. You know what kind of defense systems we need. You know how much depends on the ability to use aircraft to protect our people, our freedom [sic] aircraft that can help Ukraine, help Europe. We know they exist and you have them. They are not in Ukrainian skies.*

Zelensky then showed a brief video. It began with peacetime images of Ukrainian cities and countryside as well as smiling people of all ages. Then the images shifted to war: buildings being bombed, bodies being buried in mass graves, women and children crying. The stark contrast told everything one needed to know about Ukrainians' suffering. After the video, Zelensky concluded his remarks, this time in English, with a heartfelt plea to the American people for assistance to his country in its time of need.

> *In the end, to be the leader of the world means to be the leader of peace. Peace in your country does not depend only on you and your people. It depends on those next to you, on those who are strong. Strong does not mean weak. Strong is brave and ready to fight for his citizens as citizens of the world. For human rights. For freedom. The right to live decently and die when your time comes and not when decided by somebody else.*

Zelensky received a bipartisan standing ovation from members of Congress.

PLAYING TO THE NATION

Throughout the crisis, Zelensky assumed the role of a leader through his presence. It seemed the "role of a lifetime."[19] Zelensky fit the part, not through artifice, but through his commitment to remain in Kyiv. Specifically, he did the following:

Project concern. Russia has much more weaponry and troops than Ukraine. Prior to the February invasion, Zelensky let his country and the West know the severity of the situation. However, he did not tone down in his rhetoric. He hoped for and spoke about avoiding conflict till the actual assault began. In fact, he was critical of the United States intelligence bulletins that predicted war. He was concerned about the economic consequences about possible war.

Listen fiercely. Zelensky knew the courage of his people. They were not about to bow to Russian aggression without a fight. Zelensky listened to their hearts, which were reflected in his words and actions.

Project courage. Zelensky rallied his people against the Russian invasion of his country. Zelensky posted videos of himself remaining in Kyiv and standing with his people. We also saw videos of him meeting and mingling with his troops. Despite being the number one target of the Russians, Zelensky stayed in Kyiv during the assault on the city, regularly giving updates on the siege and vowing to remain in the city. "The fighting continues in many cities and districts of our state, but we know that we are protecting the country, the land, the future of children."[20]

Praise your people. Zelensky embraced the role of his countrymen. He praised their courage. "We won't put down our weapons," Zelensky said. "We will protect our country because our weapon is our truth and it is our land, our country, our children and we will defend all of it." [21]

RIGHTEOUS CAUSE

Not every leader—including those cited above—gets it right every time, but good leaders keep focused on bringing people together for a common cause. "We must always take sides," wrote Nobel Peace Prize winner Elie Wiesel. "Neutrality helps the oppressor, never the victim. Silence encourages the tormentor, never the tormented."[22]

Leaders inspire others to take action because it is the right thing to do. This righteousness emerges from the shared values integral to the vision and mission of the organization.

CONSIDERATIONS:

- How can you be direct and honest with your people?
- What can you do to become a better listener? What steps can you take to ensure that you understand other people's points of view?
- What can you do to recognize the achievements of people on your team?
- How can you enable your people to feel that what they do matters?

What Leaders Do to Make Things Better

In 1961, President John F. Kennedy said in his inaugural address, "The torch has been passed to a new generation of Americans."[23]

Every year brings new ideas, new challenges, and new opportunities. None of the good can occur without the active participation of leaders at every level. For that reason, leaders need to consider how to bring people together.

KNOW THE LANDSCAPE.

Facts too often fall flat at the feet of misinformation. While there are malign forces that perpetrate falsity for personal gain, there are also benign beings who cannot discern fact from fiction. It will fall to leaders to recognize the truth and propagate it as a means of solidifying logic and reason as well as strengthening the culture.

STRIVE FOR CONSENSUS, BUT DON'T BECOME HAMSTRUNG BY IT.

In indigenous cultures, the final word belongs to the man or woman who holds the title of chief. Their responsibility is to know their people and listen to them, but when final decisions about significant issues are to be made, they have the ultimate word. Same for organizations. Delegate decision-making to every level but give the voice of upholding the mission to the man or woman in charge.

SET THE RIGHT EXAMPLE.

Followers are looking for leaders who live their values. One of the reasons for the trust gap between senior executives and employees is the perception—reinforced, sadly, by the facts—that there are two sets of rules: ones for those at the top and another for those below. Living the example means being accountable and transparent.

BE INVOLVED.

Look for ways to make a difference. That starts with being there for others. Being there can be as simple as the willingness to sit and listen or as challenging as reordering an entire organization to make it more efficient as well as more accountable, transparent, and humane.

INNOVATE, THEN INNOVATE SOME MORE.

While predictions are often faulty, we can be confident that the pace of change is accelerating. It will fall to leaders to enable their organizations to think differently as well as act differently when it comes to remaining competitive. Embrace technology, yes, but also embrace the value of people. Trust them to suggest ways to innovate.

LISTEN TO YOUNGER VOICES.

Experience brings wisdom, but knowledge is not always accrued chronologically. That is, make a practice of learning from those with the least amount of tenure—short on tenure, yes, but not short on the expertise they have gained from their education, their training, and their life experiences.

LIVE WITH GRACE.

Our world is a cruel place, but it is also a place filled with kindness and joy. Leaders who seek to connect authentically with others must learn to listen with an open heart, learn with an open mind, and live with imperfection. Life is never perfect, but we can enjoy it as it is as well as seek to change what we can change for the better.

We seek to create community where individuals feel empowered to lead with conviction rooted in wisdom, compassion gained from suffering, and good examples learned from experience.

CONSIDERATIONS:

- What expectations does your team have of you as their leader?
- How can you challenge your team to think "out of the box?"
- What will you do to seek out the younger voices on your team?

Grief: The Process of Coping with Loss

"The fact that something has happened to a million other people diminishes neither grief nor joy."[24]

We humans are resilient creatures. When adversity strikes, we may pause a beat, but typically we figure out ways to overcome, or at least cope with, the new challenges.

There is an exception to our ability to bounce back.

Grief!

Grief, chiefly due to the loss of a loved one, can be debilitating, both mentally and physically. In the aftermath of the pandemic, grief is more apparent. We lost people we know, often unexpectedly.

Grief: A Brief History of Research on How Body, Mind, and Brain Adapt, by psychologist Mary-Frances O'Connor, delineates how grief affects us. As summarized in a newsletter by the Institute of Coaching (IOC), the paper discusses the psychological and physiological effects of grief. These include (and are quoted here)

- Loss of an ability to regulate emotions such as sadness and anger
- Coping by alternating between living without the individual and learning how to do so
- Loss of one's own personhood due to the loss of a loved one[25]

Rabbi Earl Grollman, who counseled survivors of the Oklahoma City bombings, writes, "Grief is not a disorder, a disease or a sign of weakness. It is an emotional, physical, and spiritual necessity, the price you pay for love. The only cure for grief is to grieve." The good news is that a majority of people recover from grief, but in other cases where there are complicating emotional and physiological factors, grief can produce degrees of clinical depression.[26]

GRIEF AFFECTS THE BODY TOO

Physiological impacts are real. For example, the "broken heart" syndrome is not a myth; acute grief can affect the immune and cardiac systems. Sometimes there is also comorbidity. The loss of a loved one contributes to the death of the spouse. And in some cases, there can be cognitive decline, especially when other factors compound grief.

There is another kind of grief produced by the loss of colleagues. Many companies have either gone out of business or laid off employees. Those left behind feel a degree of survivor's guilt—why them and not me? They also miss the camaraderie of these colleagues. There is a degree of grief; while not as acute as the loss of a loved one, there is the pain of separation.

COPING WITH GRIEF

Carol Kauffman, Ph.D., a Harvard psychologist and renowned executive coach, says executives have a role to play when it comes to grief in the workplace: "Acknowledge its presence." She advises leaders to do the opposite of a famous saying. "Don't just do something, sit there!" In other words, as Dr. Kauffman explains, "Allow the person to have their feelings."[27]

It is important to recognize such feelings. Talking about what has been lost is an acknowledgment that things have changed. It is essential to air one's feelings. It's part of the coping and eventual healing process.

Dr. Kauffman recalls an experience early in her clinical training. She related to her supervisor that her client was crying. The supervisor then asked, "What were they feeling?" Tears are an expression of emotion; crying can mean different things to different people. The challenge is to allow the individual to express themselves. So when dealing with an employee who has suffered a loss, Dr. Kauffman advises asking, "How are you holding up?" That question opens the door to conversation, and ideally a moment of sharing between individuals.

Coaches working with those who have suffered loss must understand the implications of grief to better address any adverse side effects. It is essential to maintain a healthy lifestyle through diet, exercise, and stress reduction. These factors can improve some of the symptoms. Likewise, executives who have employees experiencing grief need to be alert to the ill effects.

SOCIAL DISTANCING

Sometimes we cannot be physically present for a colleague suffering grief. We can, however, make it known that we care. We can do that by staying in touch via video chat and other forms of e-communication.

Dr. Kauffman invokes something called the "Platinum Rule."[28] That is, "Treat others as they would like to be treated, not necessarily as you would want to be treated." Dr. Kauffman continues, "Normalize in your own head, as well as in theirs, that what they're going through is normal for them." It is important to realize "that people have very different psychological needs." Individuals process grief as well as crises in different ways.[29]

Grief is real. Acknowledging it is essential. "When you can feel the grief," says Dr. Kauffman, "you are connecting with yourself in a way that is healing." Those in leadership positions must be aware of its effects and make space for those suffering from it.[30]

Grief unites us in a sense of community. We will all suffer it at one time or another. Preparing for it will enable us to cope more effectively when it strikes us.

CONSIDERATIONS:

- What do I miss most about my previous life, prior to the pandemic?
- How is my team coping with loss, e.g., colleagues, camaraderie, identity?
- What can I do to ease the grief of my colleagues?

Lead with Empathy

Empathy is the capacity to feel for someone else, to express concern for what they are experiencing. When people are suffering, they want to know that someone cares.

When we see images of people who have suffered or are caring for those suffering, we feel sympathy. We are in synchronicity with their loss. That is fine, but it's not empathy. Empathy, as classically defined in Webster's Dictionary, is "the ability to share in another's emotions, thoughts or feelings."

Leaders can be empathetic, but feeling empathy is not enough. Acting with empathy is what's necessary. "The most beautiful people we have known are those who have known defeat, known suffering, known struggle, known loss, and have found their way out of the depths," wrote the Swiss psychiatrist Elizabeth Kubler-Ross. "These persons have an appreciation, a sensitivity, and an understanding of life that fills them with compassion, gentleness, and a deep loving concern. Beautiful people do not just happen."[31]

MAKING EMPATHY REAL

To act on empathy, consider the following:

Listen intently. While sympathy is an inclination to experience another's pain, empathy is the willingness to act. You can only act if you know what the issue is. That comes from listening. Focus on the other person. Have a conversation.

Anticipate the need. Acting on empathy means not waiting to be asked. Sense the need and fulfill it. Don't ask if someone is hungry. Bring them a meal. Don't ask if they need a job. Help them find one. Don't ask people if they feel sad. Find a moment of joy for them.

Follow up. People with genuine empathy follow up to see how those in need are doing. Sometimes all a person needs is a shoulder to lean on for support. Other times it is a blueprint for survival with assistance along the way. Checking in on people keeps you in touch. It also gives the individual being helped the opportunity to say thank you. Being grateful opens the door for them to maintain their dignity. And even more, it reminds them of their self-worth.

NEED FOR COMPASSION

Leaders must do more than feel empathy; they must express it. The outward expression of empathy is compassion.

Evan Harrel, cofounder of the Center for Compassionate Leadership, told me in an interview that compassion "is the awareness of the suffering of others, coupled with the desire to help relieve that suffering."[32] As Harrel and cofounder Laura Berland believe, compassion requires more than sympathy. It requires action. "Compassionate leadership is bringing that compassion to the teams you work with" and "creating cultures of compassion so that you help remove the causes of suffering."[33]

"If we have no peace," Mother Theresa once said, "it is because we have forgotten that we belong to each other."[34] Disagreements divide us. Compassion strengthens the bonds between us. However, saying so does not make it so. It is hard, very hard, to abide others who seek to profit by dividing us. Compassion, therefore, has limits. Focus your energies on where you can make a positive difference. The way you listen to others is a window into your heart and can, in turn, open doors of understanding.

A benefit of compassion, as Berland and Harrell say, is transformation. When we experience personal upheaval, we have the opportunity to rethink who we are and how we want to live our lives. Infusing empathy with a spirit of compassion transforms how we think of our world by acting with compassion to build stronger and more inclusive communities.

CONSIDERATIONS:

- What will I do to understand what my people are experiencing?
- How will I make things better for others?

Laughter Is an Affirmation of Our Humanity

What Groucho Marx is to the Marx Brothers is what laughter is to humor. Groucho was the spark that catalyzed the comedy mayhem that made the Marx Brothers laugh-out-loud funny.

Humor is the condition of being or seeing funny things. Laughter is the physical manifestation of it.

Laughs take many forms: a chuckle, a giggle, a guffaw, a belly laugh. Humor is an elixir, a tonic that is good for mind and spirit. Laughter is good for the body.

"Some early research suggests that humor and laughter activate our bodies to turn down the stress hormones (cortisol and epinephrine) and turn up the happiness hormones (oxytocin and dopamine) as well as the natural pain killers (endorphins)," says Dr. David Fessell, a professor of radiology at the University of Michigan. More systematic research is needed, Dr. Fessell says, "But many believe the positive emotions associated with humor and laughter help decrease stress, and may help decrease the risk of stress-related diseases."[35]

During a crisis, people feel frazzled as well as pushed and pulled in different directions. In short, they need to find relief, and if they can discover that relief in a shared experience, laughter becomes more than a palliative; it becomes a unifier.

BUILDING MORALE

A historical example is *The Wipers Times*, an ersatz newspaper put together by British soldiers fighting in Flanders during World War I. (The paper took its name from the mispronunciation of the Flemish town Ypres.)

The paper, as recounted in Wikipedia, reported on the doings of the soldiers as they battled terror on the one hand and boredom on the other. Lack of access to alcohol and female company, of course, was *de rigueur*. The paper served as a relief valve for the men to vent their frustrations through humor.[36] Most British army units also staged makeshift musical reviews that played their hardships for laughs as well as provided opportunities for the troops to listen to songs that reminded them of their sweethearts back home.

A successor-in-spirit to such shows is the United Service Organizations (USO), which began in 1941 just before US involvement in World War II and continues to this day. Big-name entertainers, beginning with Bob Hope and Bing Crosby, volunteered their services. Hope made it an annual Christmastime tradition to visit the troops. Comedy was the staple, but so too were skits and music. Laughter in times of crisis is essential to morale.

LAUGHTER AS THERAPY

"Humor and laughter help us cope," says Dr. Fessell. "It helps us personally—with our mood, and likely has some positive effects on our body. And it helps us build and strengthen social bonds." It is those bonds and relationships that leaders can employ to bring the team together.

"We can use humor to reframe stressful events positively and empower ourselves. When we laugh, we remind ourselves that we are not defeated, we have agency and choice," says Dr. Fessell. "Use humor to help yourself and others laugh. If you see a funny meme, picture, or joke—share it. When you share, you create a communal spirit and that helps the team weather the storm of crisis and change."

In short, laughing together enhances cohesion and community, something we can all use in tough times.

CONSIDERATIONS:

- What can I do today to find humor in our situation?
- How does laughter make my team feel?
- What can we do together to laugh more?

Part 2

TAKE CARE OF YOURSELF

© 2016 Ted Goff

"Inhale deeply. Exhale. Relax.
We failed to meet our quota.
Inhale deeply. Exhale. Relax."

The team needs you to be your best.
Go slow to go fast.
Flex to adapt.
Eat right. Sleep more.
Put family first and make good friends and family.
Reflect more on where you are and where you want to go.
Be your best to act your best for self and for others.
Make this your finest hour!

Reinventing the "New Normal"

To survive you must take the long view. To focus on deprivation erodes the spirit. "Do not let what you cannot do interfere with what you can do," wrote legendary basketball coach John Wooden.[37] What that means in a practical sense is this: ignore what you cannot control but work on what you can control—namely yourself. The challenge is to create a workplace where people feel they belong and where they feel they can collaborate in a sense of shared community.

Focus on the now. What am I doing right now? Am I focusing on what I have lost or am I more focused on how I can get it back? Or should I even get anything back? Is it worth the struggle? Yes, you need a job. Yes, you need family and friends. What else is important to you?

Recharge or renew? The question gets to the heart of how you will spend your time now. Do you want to continue in your current career? If so, find ways to get better at what you do. Learn to use virtual media to communicate, connect, persuade, and influence. If you want to change careers, then figure out what's next. How will you prepare yourself to do something else—schooling, training, or acquiring new skills?

Orient yourself to the future. The "new normal" is evolving. We are all explorers in this new world. We are akin to the men Columbus took with him on a voyage to what was planned to be the Far East. Instead, he found a world unknown to Europeans. This "discovery" created new opportunities for the travelers but destroyed the civilizations that were already present. Our challenge is to adjust to the unexpected, cope with the changes as a means of creating a future that benefits the whole, not merely the few.

Anchor yourself. No one knows what tomorrow will bring but you can bet that what we have always held dear will remain. The virtues that shape us—integrity, trust, and love—will remain. We need to remember to hold on to them.

Hardship steels the spine. Knowing what you can do and doing it will steel the soul as well as the spine.

CONSIDERATIONS:

- How am I allowing my people (and myself) to mourn what we have lost?
- What am I doing to recharge myself?
- What am I doing to renew my spirit?
- How am I thinking about the future?
- How are my values helping me move ahead?

How Leaders Flex in a Crisis

Leaders often do not choose their issues. Issues choose them.

George W. Bush wanted his presidency to focus on "education policy and domestic affairs." As John Dickerson writes in *The Hardest Job in the World: The American Presidency*, "the word 'terrorism' came up only once, and in passing" during three presidential debates in 2000. Eight months into his first term, Bush was dealing with the 9/11 attacks. As Dickerson notes, foreign policy so defined his presidency that President Barack Obama ran against Bush's notion of an "arrogant foreign policy."[38]

Obama, like Bush, wanted to focus on domestic policy. In September of 2008, it was clear that improving things for America would require rebuilding the economy, which was just entering the Great Recession.

It is not only issues that leaders face; it's velocity. "The urgent should not crowd out the important," Dickerson quotes former Obama aide Lisa Monaco. "But sometimes you don't get to the important. Your day is spent just trying to prioritize the urgent. Which is urgent first?"

Those quotes resonate today with most leaders because the last few months have been a tsunami of change. Corporate leaders in January had a rosy outlook for the economy. It was an election year, after all. No one in public administration was thinking about closing administrative and judicial offices. Who in education considered closing school doors and opening virtual windows?

EVERYTHING HAS CHANGED

When significant changes and crises occur, leaders do not get to choose one or the other; they must deal with all of them. Simultaneously.

So how do leaders do it? The easy answer is to prioritize—but prioritize what, when everything is important? Well, executives need to focus on the mission. What do they deliver to others—customers or constituents—and how can they keep on doing it?

Relevancy is critical. Executives need to continue to evaluate their business models in response to changing conditions. This model can also be applied to social justice. Just as organizations rethink what they offer, they need to consider how they provide and treat their employees. How can they become more inclusive? Yes, it's the right thing to do, but it's also the smart thing to do. The more you are like your customers, the greater understanding you can have and the more responsive you can be.

Once certainty of today is that the "new normal" is forever being invented. What you do today may not be sustainable tomorrow. What is sustainable is enabling your people to help respond to changing conditions. No executive has all the answers. She is only as capable as her team. Her challenge is to make it safe for people to try new things, and yes, to fail, but to continue to respond in ways that enable the enterprise to move forward.

CONSIDERATIONS:

- What will you do to improve your focus?
- How can you become more agile?
- How can you repurpose your organization?

How to Lead during a Crisis

Crises occur with regularity. We may not be aware of when or how they will occur, but we do know they will happen. The challenge for leaders is to prepare in advance so you know what you will do when a crisis strikes.

Look before you leap. The urge to act with alacrity surfaces in times of turmoil. Speed should dictate how you react to a crisis, but not necessarily a post-crisis. Consider your alternatives. Be thoughtful and deliberate. What you imagined was essential before the crisis struck may not be so critical after all.

Roll the dice. Draw up your assumptions. Test them, however, with a combination of research and common sense. Then make your decision according to the probabilities. What was once an 80/20 proposition may now be 50/50. There is more uncertainty now.

Slow down. How can that be possible? With changes that roll us one day and roil us the next, the urge to keep moving is strong. But, unless moving immediately is necessary due to cash-flow, take time to reflect. Consider your strengths as well as your shortcomings. How are you using what you do best to overcome what you do worst? Be mindful of what you have and ask for help whenever you can.

Seek mutuality. Gone is our time of winner take all. Now we must cultivate an attitude of "winner share all." Look for solutions that benefit others more than yourself. Find ways to lift people up rather than hold them down. Leaders, of course, abide by this creed, but in our upside-down world, that abundance can be shared. Doing so increases the bounty for all. It reinforces the need for, and importance of, community.

CONSIDERATIONS:

- What steps can you take to become more deliberate?
- How will you ensure you make time to "slow things down?"
- What can you to do craft win-win solutions?

Apply Resilience to Stress

No two people respond to adversity the same way.

Some folks embrace the challenge and figure things out for themselves. Others—the majority of us—need help from experts to navigate the problems we are facing related to stress and fear. One expert I have turned to is Sharon Melnick, Ph.D., a leading authority on stress resilience who did a decade's worth of research work at Harvard Medical School.

Some managers may think that they do not have time to coach their people. "The leader doesn't have time to 'not do this,'" Dr. Melnick told me in an email interview. "All the research prior to this crisis indicates that employees who feel a sense of belonging and psychological safety will be engaged with the work and have loyalty to the manager and organization."[39]

"Managers want to remember that the work gets done through people," says Dr. Melnick. A manager can alleviate stress through conversation. "That will help the employee spend more time on the work. And it will make that employee so much more motivated to work for that manager." Or, as Dr. Melnick says, "Going slow to go fast."[40]

Dr. Melnick's book, *Success Under Stress: Powerful Tools for Staying Calm, Confident and Productive When the Pressure's On*, is a useful resource for any manager wondering how to manage his own fears, let alone deal with the stress his employees are feeling. With Dr. Melnick's permission, I have pulled out some practical wisdom nuggets from a guide she adapted from her book.[41]

Demonstrate optimism rooted in reality. When the world is coming apart, how can anyone be optimistic? "Optimism paints a positive mental picture of the future and implies there is something that each team member can do to help adapt and achieve success," writes Dr. Melnick. "It communicates your belief in your team, activates problem-solving abilities, and has even been shown to maintain healthy immune functioning." It is critical to ground optimism in the truth, however discomforting it may be. False promises undermine a leader's credibility.[42]

Learn to balance your body's ON/OFF systems. "When you are ON, adrenaline helps you problem solve and carry out all the tasks of your day," says Dr. Melnick. "Because everything feels like a priority, we tend to use our ON system and push ourselves all day."[43] Dr. Melnick writes in her guidebook, "This ON system is extremely useful for quick responses and tactical tasks, but we can make thinking mistakes like over-focusing on the problem or doing business as usual just to get it done expediently."[44]

Dr. Melnick advises that you need your OFF system to engage in strategic thinking and innovation. It is for this reason that executives may rush big decisions without taking time to deliberate beforehand. "With ongoing stress, it is important to activate that OFF system whenever you can," says Dr. Melnick. "Taking mental breaks—getting away from what you are doing if only for a short period of time—is rejuvenating."[45]

One technique Dr. Melnick teaches is a breathing exercise. "Exhale for longer than you inhale. Breathe in for three counts, out for six counts. This kind of breathing can calm your mind quickly." Another way to concentrate more fully is through mindfulness. Practicing it can be as simple as "slowing down your attention and focusing on the moment-to-moment tasks."[46]

Communicate regularly. Lack of control makes people stressed. Keep your people in the loop. Share information as much as you can. Dr. Melnick advises keeping directions short and to the point and repeating directions often. When stress levels are high, people cannot absorb great quantities of information, and they forget. For this reason, it's also important to listen to your people. Empathize with their feelings of stress so they trust you and will follow your direction.

Keep your team's spirits up. Things will go wrong. People will make mistakes. Be careful how you respond. Dr. Melnick writes, "Remind them they are doing their best under the circumstances. Encourage them to have someone who is safe to talk to about their sense of overwhelm, so they don't have to internalize the stress while putting up a tough front."

Feeling stress is a human condition. So too is resilience. Applying techniques we gain from others, coupled with our own inner resolve, will enable us to manage it more effectively and, in turn, lead more capably and humanely. [47]

CONSIDERATIONS:

- What steps can you take to reduce stress at work?
- What steps can you take to reduce stress at home?

Open Your Eyes to Your Blind Spots

"It is vital to recognize that bias is generated reflexively by the brain, and masquerades as reality. As a distortion, bias blocks our access to the present reality. When our biases are in charge, we are on automatic pilot and unaware of the uniqueness of the present moment and other people."[48]

So concludes a summary newsletter article on the topic of bias produced by the Institute of Coaching. Direct and straightforward, the above statement gets to the heart of the matter. Bias is within us, and so much so we often do not recognize it because it distorts our reality.

Fortunately, this report—which is based upon research by American social psychologist Jennifer Eberhardt and the book *Sway: Unravelling Unconscious Bias* by Pragya Agarwal—asserts that bias is not terminal. "Bias can then be deconstructed over time through new social experiences: positive examples and role models, and positive experiences and relationships with out-group members."[49]

WIDE-RANGING ILL EFFECTS

The effects of discrimination are insidious and corrosive. Those in the "out-group" experience the following effects that are emotionally, physically, and spiritually degrading. As noted in the report (and quoted here), these negative factors include:

- Being slighted—feeling invisible, not being treated respectfully as individuals, being quickly judged and categorized
- Lacking a sense of belonging and inclusion, reduced self-esteem and connection
- Fearing discrimination, which leads to stress, anxiety, and self-consciousness
- Impaired cognitive processing and performance caused by stress, reducing competence and confidence
- Inflammation and chronic disease, both physical and mental illness brought on by chronic stress and causing physical suffering and shorter lifespans
- Internalizing bias so that it becomes self-fulfilling

OVERCOMING BIAS

Ridding oneself of bias takes diligence and effort. Jonathan Swift, an Anglo-Irish satirist born in 1667, captured today's dilemma perfectly. "It is useless to attempt to reason a man out of a thing he was never reasoned into."[50] First, you need to recognize that bias is part of the human condition. We are attuned to what we know, and when we encounter individuals and cultures different from our own, we make judgments. We are acting on bias.

Practical steps to mitigating bias include the willingness to confront it through reflection as well as education. Reflect upon what you know and what you don't know. Consider how you have acted with bias in the past and how that bias may have harmed others. Most importantly, recognize that bias hurts the self, too. Living within a cocoon of assumptions is limiting and shortsighted. Discrimination erodes an individual's ability to separate fact from fiction. A closed mind leads to a closed heart.

Eliminating bias also requires courage. If you have always made assumptions about people based on what you think is true, but in reality, it is not, you must confront the fact that you have been wrong. Admitting a mistake takes guts, especially if you have been overt in your misperceptions.

Change begins within each of us. Our challenge is to be the example we wish to become. That is, consider how you can listen more carefully, read more broadly, think before you speak, and, most importantly, avoid the "not me" syndrome. Each of us has biases. Failure to recognize them is a weakness. Resolving to overcome them makes us stronger.

In her memoir, *Becoming*, former First Lady Michelle Obama wrote:

> Let's invite one another in. Maybe then we can begin to fear less, to make fewer wrong assumptions, to let go of the biases and stereotypes that unnecessarily divide us. Maybe we can better embrace the ways we are the same. It's not about being perfect. It's not about where you get yourself in the end. There's power in allowing yourself to be known and heard, in own-

ing your unique story, in using your authentic voice. And there's grace in being willing to know and hear others. This, for me, is how we become.[51]

History is full of people who have confronted their own bias and, in doing so, came to a greater sense of themselves. It gave them confidence in their abilities to build a better culture—one where people feel a sense of belonging to the community, not apart from it.

CONSIDERATIONS:

- What are the biggest factors hurting people in your organization?
- What can you do to remove obstacles to fair treatment?
- How will you ensure you are keeping on track?

If Honesty Is the Best Policy, Why Do We Forget It?

Be honest!

That's the sentiment that my friend John U. Bacon, bestselling author and sports commentator, expressed in a commentary for Michigan Radio. Bacon was referencing advice from the University of Michigan's former sports information director, Bruce Madej, who said, "First, let's start with the truth."[52] While the advice is simple it is often ignored, and it leads to a failure of integrity.

Being honest about wrongdoing requires courage. The reason that organizations, large and small, for-profit and non-profit, get into trouble, is that too often when a crisis strikes, the instinct is to protect the institution before addressing the harm done to its victims.

There is another aspect of honesty: tell people what they need to hear. During a crisis, people are upset; they seek reassurance. A leader who delivers the truth and does so calmly and confidently gives people a reason to believe that the right people are in charge and will do what they can to improve the situation. At the same time, honesty dictates being straight with people. Just because they seek comfort does not mean you dispense bromides like "everything will be better, trust me." No, be brutally honest.

A HISTORY LESSON

A classic example of brutal honesty was Franklin Roosevelt's address to Congress and the nation on December 8, 1941, the day after the Japanese navy's attack on Pearl Harbor. While we remember his comments as the "Day of Infamy" speech, we forget the tenor and tone of his voice. It was firm and resolute. After excoriating Japanese aggression, Roosevelt did not pull any punches. Although he did not reveal the full damage done to the US Navy, he did not sugarcoat the losses.[53]

"The attack yesterday on the Hawaiian Islands has caused severe damage to American naval and military forces. I regret to tell you that very many American lives have been lost. In addition, American ships have been reported torpedoed on the high seas between San Francisco and Honolulu."

Then, Roosevelt asserted his leadership and his faith in our military.

"As Commander in Chief of the Army and Navy, I have directed that all measures be taken for our defense. But always will our whole nation remember the character of the onslaught against us."

Roosevelt lastly turned what had happened on this "Day of Infamy" into a righteous cause for all Americans.

"No matter how long it may take us to overcome this premeditated invasion, the American people in their righteous might will win through to absolute victory."

Leaders need to keep connected to their people. Here are some suggestions to build greater levels of trust.

Avoid sugarcoating. Be straight with people. Reveal what you can about the business, but do not make promises you cannot keep, e.g., no layoffs. Stick to the facts. And remember that even what you think is valid now may not be so tomorrow.

Stay connected. Whether your employees are in the workplace or working from home, make yourself available. In times of change, stress levels rise. Listen to their concerns. Be open to help when you can.

Take care. The stress on leaders now is enormous. Uncertainty weighs heavily. There is often a tendency to push aside personal concerns. But if you are in charge, you must make certain you eat right, get enough sleep, and exercise when you can. Getting outside for a quick walk not only provides you with some exercise, but it can also give you a break to clear your head.

In the novel *The Kite Runner*, author Khaled Hosseini writes, "When you tell a lie, you steal someone's else's right to the truth."[54] Honesty raises a cause to righteousness. Dishonesty not only taints the leader but also erodes faith in the institution. When people lose confidence in their leader, they also turn away from that institution. By contrast, as seen from Roosevelt's actions, when people believe in their leader, they join in community with him to put things right.

Better to face an ugly reality immediately than to have it rot. Be honest.

CONSIDERATIONS:

- Why is it difficult to tell the truth?
- What have you seen that makes you want to speak the truth?

Yes, Leadership Is an Act
(and That's Not Bad!)

"Never perform with your heart not being in it. Never allow yourself to get to the point where it's a job. Always make sure that your spirit is focused so that communicating music to other people is a central priority for you."

That's what pianist and conductor Michael Tilson Thomas told Terry Gross on NPR's *Fresh Air* about his approach to playing music. Tilson Thomas was recently named a Kennedy Center Honors recipient of the lifetime achievement in the arts.[55]

Good entertainers know what Tilson Thomas means instinctively. They deliver their material in ways that seem alive and new, even though they have done the song, a bit, or a monologue a thousand times before. The good ones inject it with life, even when they are not feeling it. The same goes for athletes. Seldom does a pro take the field or the court and feel tip-top. No, they have aches and pains, as well as distractions in their heads. But they put it all aside and deliver.

That's a lesson for anyone in a leadership position. You have to bring your heart and spirit to the job. People know when you are going through the motions. One vivid example brings this concept into sharp focus.

When Alan Mulally was CEO of Ford Motor Company, he often did "grip and grin" pictures with members of the franchise dealer network, all independent businesspeople. It's a common practice, and most CEOs do it, but sometimes reluctantly, complete with a plastic smile and limp handshake. Not Mulally—he plunged into the task with a full heart and plenty of spirit.

To everyone who came to have their picture taken with him, Mulally asked questions about their business. He posed carefully, even asking the photographer if it looked right. After the snap was taken, he grinned or laughed and patted them on the back. Mulally did this not a few times, not twenty times, not a hundred times…but over five hundred times. In one night. And, he did it again on subsequent nights with different groups of dealers.

BRING YOUR TECHNIQUE TO YOUR LEADERSHIP

That's bringing your heart to the game. Doing something repeatedly takes commitment as well as technique. Leaders in public—and these days public can mean anything from the cafeteria to a testimony at city hall or the halls of Congress—must be aware they are on stage. And as performers, they must act. So, here are some techniques to employ.

Prepare in advance. What do followers want from you? Maybe it's a presentation or a handshake. Or it could be a special message about what's happening at headquarters? Deliver what's expected, as well as be ready for surprises. Some people may want to take a verbal swing at you, so be prepared for it.

Take it in stride. Listen to what they say. Answer them respectfully. You may not satisfy them immediately, but you will have demonstrated that you have heard the complaint.

Keep your chin up. Days get long, especially when you are doing something repetitious like shaking hands or meeting and mingling with new employees. Understand something: to them, you are special. So, act the part. Act like the person in charge they want you to be.

Find joy. Look for opportunities to compliment employees on what they have accomplished. Stay in the moment and look people in the eye when you meet them. Smile when appropriate. Relish opportunities to share a laugh.

Might skeptics say, isn't he or she faking it? Sure they are, just as actors or ballplayers do night after night. They are not feeling 100 percent every time or even every other time. They rely on their technique. So too can leaders in public.

Legendary acting teacher Sanford Meisner once said, "Acting is behaving truthfully under imaginary circumstances." Adjusted for leaders, we might say, "Leading is behaving truthfully under real circumstances." Truth comes from behaving honestly and with integrity. Such truths cause people to pay attention and allow you to lead them in a sense of shared purpose and common good.[56]

CONSIDERATIONS:

- What gives you joy?
- What about your team gives you hope for the future?
- How can ensure there is joy in the workplace?

Be Willing to Embrace Personal Change

"Let's get to work."

That's how former President Barack Obama closed his essay in *Medium* that summarized his thinking on the recent unrest provoked by the killing of George Floyd by a Minneapolis police officer.[57] One thought in particular which the former president expressed caught my attention:

> So the bottom line is this: if we want to bring about real change, then the choice isn't between protest and politics. *We have to do both*. We have to mobilize to raise awareness, *and* we have to organize and cast our ballots to make sure that we elect candidates who will act on reform.[58]

Protesting injustice and voting for reform candidates do work. The civil rights movement of the 1950s and '60s effected real change. It may not seem so today when you turn on cable news, but take a step back and look at the faces you see—not just protestors, but mayors, police chiefs, prosecutors and, yes, reporters. They are women and men of color. Their positions of power and influence came as a direct result of the protests and politics fostered by their grandparents and parents.

There is more work to do. For that to occur, more change is necessary. Mobilization on the streets and at the ballot box helps affect that change. But that is not enough. In the workplace, it is not enough to hire more minorities; it is a matter of practicing inclusion. The goal is to give everyone an equitable opportunity to demonstrate his or her talents and skills in order to gain opportunities for advancement. Such changes can only occur when we dare to look inside ourselves and examine our own lives.

ACKNOWLEDGE THE NEED TO CHANGE

Change only begins with an acknowledgment of our shortcomings. As human beings, we are the sum of our beliefs, practices, and yes, biases. Only when we recognize such preferences will we begin to see people different from us as people, not stereotypes.

When it comes to bias, I know I have been guilty of seeing others who are different from me with a closed mind. I, too, have made presumptions about others. I want to think I have outgrown such biases, but I know that if I am honest with myself, while I have discarded those biases, I have assumed others. I acknowledge this shortcoming as a means of affirming my frailties. I, like many of us, am a work in progress.

The challenge for each of us is to find ways to connect more authentically with others. Doing so melts biases because we see others for who they indeed are rather than who we presume they are. We see them as reflections of ourselves, truly human and possessed of the same strengths and, in some cases, the same biases, that we hold.

So how do we do this? How can we change ourselves? That is a big question upon which books—in fact, bookshelves and bookcases full of books—have been written. Distilling this knowledge into practical steps requires that we begin with a few building-block questions.

- **Why do I want to change?** We want to switch to become more fully human, to see others as we see ourselves, as people more like us than different from us.
- **What is holding me back from change?** We resist because our biases—often ingrained through years of practice—keep us back from seeing other people for what they are: human beings, not stereotypes.
- **How can I make the change?** We change because we *want* to change. To do that, we can call upon the goodness that exists within each of us. I call it grace.

CATALYST FOR CHANGE

Grace, as I define it, is that catalyst for the greater good that we activate when we want to make positive change. Grace facilitates change, but it does not make it permanent. Only we can make it permanent by behaving in ways that demonstrate good intentions that result in positive outcomes.

Change is never easy. Ultimately, as many have said, we change because it hurts too much not to change. Such hurt permeates our current situation. We are tired of seeing Black women and men viewed as suspects first, people second. We are bothered by a culture that divides people according to ethnicity and culture. And finally, we are weary of living in a society where bigotry corrodes our national discourse.

We are better than this. But we can only become better if we commit to making changes that are specific and actionable. So, consider the following.

- Assume the best in others. Yes, we all have something useful to offer one another.
- Turn negative thoughts into positive ones. Prejudice thrives in negativity.
- Look to build community with others with whom you might not always agree to strengthen the common good.

Finally, recognize that what you do now matters. Failing to do anything ensures that nothing will change. Committing to act differently provides different outcomes—not perfect outcomes, but better ones.

CONSIDERATIONS:

- Consider the three questions above regarding change. What will you do differently?
- What can you do now to assume the best intentions of others?
- What volunteer activities in your community could your company support?

How to Lead in a Hybrid World

Virtual is not a synonym for invisible.

What it takes to lead is timeless. Leaders lead for the betterment of others. To do this, they become a presence in the lives of those they lead. Presence once came automatically with hierarchy. There are far fewer layers of management now; managers are encouraged to make decisions without approval from on high as long as they are working within strategic imperatives. A leader's presence becomes more stretched, and in some cases more diluted.

Women managers, an oddity forty years ago, are commonplace. Not enough are in positions of the highest authority, but that too is changing as more and more women become CEOs. Women leaders excel in presence because most have a keen sense of what it means to be present in the lives of their employees.

Velocity and globalism, too, alter the leadership landscape. What happens in one part of the world can impact another within a short period of time. The global supply chain, once heralded as a breakthrough in efficiency and cost-saving, suddenly became a liability during the pandemic. Manufacturers throughout the world could not obtain microchips necessary for their products, which included everything from computers and phones to automobiles.

And that brings me to the change many millions embrace today: working from anywhere, sometimes in the office and sometimes at home. We may lack the physical presence of our boss. For some, this is a relief. But it should not be allowed to negate the need for and the imperative of a leader's presence.

Absence, as it applies to leadership, does not make the heart grow fonder. It does the opposite. When the boss is not around, people forget about him and do their own thing. They also get the feeling that the boss cares little for him and so they return the favor by caring for their company.

NEED FOR PRESENCE

Now more than ever, we need leaders to exert themselves to be seen and heard. Technology improves visibility and messaging. We are all as proximate as our nearest Zoom, Skype, or WebEx meetings. Virtual proximity, however, does not automatically equal closeness, or more importantly, connectedness.

My colleague, Ron Carucci, cofounder and managing partner of Navalent, a consultancy firm, believes that virtual leadership comes down to presence. Since we cannot be there, we must be *felt* there.[59]

Presence for leaders means being accessible to others—letting people know that you are available to listen as well as to support. A fully present leader is one who is engaged in the work and conversant with the people who do the job. Doing this virtually is not easy.

To be present in a hybrid world, the leader needs to "reach out and touch"—metaphorically speaking. When you cannot be in an office, you connect with people via text, email, and video. You "touch" them when you share yourself with them. You share your personal story and, in turn, listen to theirs. There can be an intimacy that develops between people when they are apart if they regularly stay in touch with one another.

Working in isolation can lead to feelings of dislocation and even disengagement. That is why a leader who can make her presence felt through her words and her example will be one that others want to follow and go the extra mile for—even when they are working from anywhere.

Whether we work virtually or in-person—or a combination of both—we will need leaders to guide us. Leaders who are present now through challenging times will be those who reassure us with their presence and forge a new sense of community.

CONSIDERATIONS:

- How can I make myself fully present using media?
- What can I do to make myself more accessible?

Part 3

PREPARE FOR THE FUTURE

"I feel it's important to always
have a plan to ignore."

Move forward or get out of the way.
Crises wait for no one.
You either deal with them, or they deal with you—badly.
Peer through the clouds.
Look over the horizon.
Find the path forward.
Question assumptions always.
Trust your people.
Have patience. (Don't forget to breathe.)
Act on what you know.
Lead with grace.

What Next? Create Community Now

Once upon a time, community was defined by where you lived, worshipped, and worked. Then over the years the sense of community eroded. The bonds of work slowly eroded too. People found themselves isolated and lonely.

In 2014, Christine Porath and Tony Schwartz conducted a research study of work-life issues published in the *Harvard Business Review*. Their findings showed that two-thirds of employees feel no sense of community at work.[60]

The loss of community has stuck with Porath, and she explores how we can rebuild it in her newest book, *Mastering Community: The Surprising Ways Coming Together Moves Us from Surviving to Thriving*.[61]

Porath, a professor at Georgetown University's McDonough School of Business, sees firsthand how the need for community has grown. She notes that when she first began teaching a couple of decades ago, the need for civility (the topic of her 2016 book, *Mastering Civility: A Manifesto for the Workplace*) was not a priority. However, she told me in an interview that some students feared that exerting civility would make them appear less leader-like, that it would equate to being soft and not tough enough to lead in business.[62]

Enter vulnerability. That sentiment allows us to look more deeply into how we relate to one another, especially to our leaders. With a heightened awareness of connection, the need for community grows.

THE DIVIDEND

There is a business equation to fostering a stronger sense of community. When people feel connected to their workplace, there is less turnover. That fact alone should make management sit up and take notice of people's need to be connected. In her book, *Mastering Community*, Porath tells the story of a woman who ran a call center at Dell. This manager noted that people were gaining weight, so she took it upon herself to provide exercise for her employees, including hiring a personal trainer who would conduct exercise sessions at lunchtime.

As Porath explained to me, the manager's actions accomplished two things. One, participants lost weight. Two, participants connected more effectively and as a result their performance at work improved. Porath stresses that this manager was not a senior executive; she acted on her own to foster better conditions for employees.

NURTURING COMMUNITY

Intrinsically at work, the need for community is powerful. Leaders nurture this connection by showing respect for employees, valuing them as contributors, and being candid with them about their performance. Bottomline, says Porath, "You are making people feel like they belong. I think that that's crucial to making people feel valued. One of the things that always surprises me, particularly when I get into research, is that people don't receive thanks." Showing gratitude says Porath is free and "can be done easily."

With a sense of community, "People feel this greater sense of thriving. They tend to perform better objectively as rated by bosses. They're far healthier. They have much less burnout. I think that there are a lot of potential outcomes [for the community] that speak to a much happier, more productive workforce," Porath says. Such sentiment makes the employee much more likely to stay with their employer.

MORE THAN A PLACE TO WORK

Regard your workplace as a community. Communities by nature are places where people feel they belong. It is more than a place to work; it becomes a place to be.

Father Greg Boyle, a Jesuit priest, has taken the sense of community to new heights with the organization he founded in East Los Angeles in the late eighties. It's called Homeboy Industries, and its purpose initially was to employ ex-gang members.

What binds the community together, as Father Boyle writes in his newest book, *The Whole Language: The Power of Extravagant Tenderness*, is that "Homeboy is a place of grace and chaos—where joy is always waiting in the wings."[63]

Homeboy Industries, now the largest gang intervention program globally, is where men and women who have led lives of crime—most often because they were victims of abuse and abandonment—can feel a sense of belonging. "It is only belonging, and not mere inclusion, that fully arouses bravery in others. You start with a broken heart and remove what encases it." Doing such takes great courage and what "homies" calls "tenderoni"—love, compassion, and tenderness. The lessons of Homebody Industries show the power of caring, and as such, it can teach other organizations, which have far more advantages, powerful lessons.

Lay down your baggage. Each of us is an accumulation of successes as well as failures. We have our quirks and our moods. When you belong to a community, you are not your resume. You become a fellow contributor.

Find ways to work with people unlike yourself. It is not uncommon for homies who once belonged to rival gangs to work together. It is never easy, but within the Homeboy culture, learning to get along is vital to becoming a whole person.

Build trust by showing trust. Of course, we want others to trust us, but how often do we wait for the "other person" to make the first move? Better to show others who you are first. Be open with them. Give them the benefit of the doubt.

Respect is fundamental to each step and essential to building a solid community. We reinforce respect through our actions—assisting, listening, and caring. Doing these things make colleagues feel wanted, recognized, and respected, just as we want to feel in return.

WHAT COMMUNITY ENABLES

Work takes up a considerable amount of time. Rather than viewing it as something I "go to," research by Porath and others shows that it can be something I "belong to." The sense of belonging heightens our ability to cooperate with others and collaborate in ways that enable individuals and teams more than they had expected. Community nurtures the bonds that bind us in ways that employees find more fulfilling and that employers can find more rewarding.

CONSIDERATIONS:

- What does community mean to you?
- How can you create community in your workplace?

Embrace the Unknown

"Nobody knows anything...Not one person in the entire motion picture field knows for a certainty what's going to work. Every time out, it's a guess and, if you're lucky, an educated one."

William Goldman, the novelist and Academy Award-winning screenwriter of *Butch Cassidy and the Sundance Kid, The Princess Bride*, and *All the President's Men*, wrote that in his book about Hollywood called *Adventures in the Screen Trade*. It is a reference to producers' lack of ability to predict which movies will be successful. If they were so smart, they would produce nothing but hits—which, of course, does not happen.[64]

NEW IDEAS, NEW INNOVATIONS

Nearly two dozen companies—and thousands of researchers—worked on a vaccine for Covid-19. Never before in the history of medical science have so many different teams, many from competing companies, come together to work for a common cause.

All of this reminds me of another time, the first hundred days of the administration of Franklin Roosevelt. With the nation on its knees financially, Roosevelt mobilized all resources from businesses as well as the social sector to get people back to work and to rebuild the country. The operative mantra of this time was, "Try this; try that, but by God, try something." Roosevelt initiated what was called the alphabet agencies, nick-named for their acronyms. Some things, like the Works Progress Administration (WPA), the Tennessee Valley Authority (TVA), and the Civilian Conservation Corps (CCC), had a lasting impact on our nation in building our infrastructure. Other projects have faded from memory.[65]

It was not till the mobilization for World War II that Americans were put back to work, men into the services, women into jobs formerly held by men. Yet people felt in their hearts that with Roosevelt, things would get better. Roosevelt, they felt, was listening to them.

WHAT TO DO NOW

That's what business leaders need to do: listen to their employees. None of us know what will come next, but we know we must do something. Crisis provokes innovation. The challenge is for management to enable it to be safe to try and try again. Here are a few action steps.

- Create virtual town halls where employees are encouraged to come with ideas about a given issue.
- Choose suggestions to be explored by individuals and teams.
- Execute the best ideas and keep people apprised of their progress.

- Follow up and evaluate successes.

Then rinse and repeat. Listen. Suggest. Execute. Evaluate. It is not rocket science, but it is a way to get employees engaged in the issues of the day and give them a voice in solving them.

One thing is for sure. The new normal will not be the old normal. And while we can mourn the loss of the old familiar, we can take heart that when people put their hearts and minds into something greater than themselves, good things can happen.

Two millennia ago, the Roman emperor Marcus Aurelius posited, "Never let the future disturb you. You will meet it, if you have to, with the same weapons of reason which today arm you against the present."[66]

The answers to the future lie within the talents of the people working hard today.

CONSIDERATIONS:

- Where are you now?
- What have you done that has worked? Why?
- What have you done that has not worked? Why?
- What will you do differently going forward?
- What are you doing that is hurting your team from being more creative?
- What steps can you take to enable your people to raise, discuss, and implement new ideas?
- What one or two new ideas from your team can you implement this week or this month?

How to Challenge
the Status Quo

Can we look at ourselves and our organizations objectively?

That perspective begins with questioning the status quo. "If you do not know how to ask the right question," said management theorist and consultant, W. Edwards Deming, "you discover nothing."[67] So just what are the "right questions?"

What do people say about working here? Happy talk is the detritus of every large organization. The challenge is to get people to voice their opinions about what they like and don't like about their work. Psychological safety, as Amy C. Edmondson of the Harvard Business School teaches, is the freedom to express alternate views without fear of persecution and with a sense of belonging.

How well do we practice equity and inclusion? Diversity is the untapped reservoir of talent within every organization, but too often, it is regarded as a matter of quota rather than inclusiveness. The questions that need to be asked include these: how likely are women to be promoted? What kind of recruiting are we doing to attract employees who are different from us? How are we addressing neurodiversity and tapping into its advantages?

How well are we planning for the future? Looking over the top of the building is the job of every CEO. What keeps CEOs up at night is not what they know; it's what they don't know. How prepared is the organization for shifts in the business as well as new challenges from new competitors, known and unknown?

Surveys can collect data that measure the culture both short-term and long-term. This data can provide a rich trove of information that can be shared throughout the organization. Even better, such data can form the basis for discussions with employees at all levels.

Nothing, however, can supplant the need for senior leadership to become involved. Meet, mingle, talk, and discourse with rank and file to assess how people are feeling about the here and now and the future around the corner.

Answers to these questions are those that provide insights into creating a workplace where people want to be, want to belong to, and want to contribute because they feel they are working for common goals in community of shared values. To do that requires strategic thinking. Developing a strategic view requires the following points.

Know the situation. Before you invest in the project, study the issues as well as the competition. Know what you can offer and why it matters.

Know your resources. How much can you invest? Initiatives begin with funding that often proves insufficient whether you do continue to invest or pull the plug.

Develop a strategy. What does success look like? If you can answer it quickly, then you are on the right path. If you don't know the endgame, you know that you are headed for more trouble.

Revise your strategy. When the situation changes, reexamine your approach. What do you need to do differently, and why?

None of these ideas are new or unique. The problem is we may overlook them in our rush to complete a project. The challenge for leaders is to act on the path forward, but remain vigilant to altering the path when the situation dictates.

Follow a dictum of Harvard Business School professor Michael Porter, considered a seminal thinker on strategy, who wrote, "The essence of strategy is choosing what not to do."[68]

Keep focused on the mission and align everything toward it. Avoid the distractions of the "next big thing." Strategy is a discipline, and without it, missions are destined to flounder. Organizations that bury their heads in the sand will one day be covered by it, and that won't be good for anyone or anything.

"A prudent question," wrote sixteenth century philosopher-statesman Francis Bacon, "is one-half of wisdom." A leader's challenge is to solve the other half of that equation by continuing to ask questions and act upon what she learns.[69]

CONSIDERATIONS:

- What can you do to get people to speak up about issues that concern them?
- What steps will you take to be inclusive?
- How will you encourage people to think strategically?
- How will you enable them to execute strategies?

Listen to Others Before You Decide

Presidents Dwight D. Eisenhower and John F. Kennedy were not friends, yet after the failure of the Bay of Pigs disaster in early 1961, the two began to speak. Eisenhower's administration had planned the invasion and it was executed under Kennedy's watch.

According to historian Jon Meacham's account in *Songs of America: Patriotism, Protest, and the Music That Made a Nation*, Ike asked, "Mr. President, before you approved this [plan for the invasion], did you have everybody in front of you debating the thing so you got the pros and cons yourself and then made the decision, or did you see these people one at time?" Kennedy assumed responsibility, adding, "I just took their advice."[70] (In fact, there was debate among the aides that occurred in Kennedy's presence, according to historian Mark K. Updegrove, in his book, *Incomparable Grace*. But when speaking to Eisenhower Kennedy sidestepped that issue.)[71]

Going forward, Kennedy asserted more control. He implemented ExComm (Executive Committee for the National Security Council) which was used to good effect during the

Cuban Missile Crisis in October 1962. Kennedy was able to neutralize the over-aggressive tendencies of some like General Curtis LeMay with the more moderate voices in his Cabinet. Nuclear war was averted.

Ike's question to Kennedy is a good lesson for anyone in a leadership position. While leaders do make the ultimate decision on major issues, it is best to finalize the decision after debate and deliberation. Every decision need not be debated— only those that have a significant impact on the organization. But if issues are discussed, here are some ground rules.

Convene the experts. Get the people who know the most about the issue in the same room. Give them advance notice of what will be discussed and have them prepare their arguments based on facts as well as their experience.

Set ground rules. Most importantly, make it clear that the purpose of the meeting is to consider the issue and debate it. Focus energy on the facts. Easy to say, but when one or more people in the room may be rivals, vying for an advantage with the boss, the senior person in the room must keep the discussion focused.

Decide. Often a leader will ask people for their recommendation. He or she will make it clear that the final decision lies with them due to their position. Let people know what has been decided in a timely fashion. Failure to do so leaves people hanging and the organization in stasis.

After debate and deliberation, keep individuals in the loop. Let them know the impact of the decision. Be available to listen to further suggestions but hold fast to the decision to give it time to take effect. Changes can be made later.

TIME AND DELEGATION

The debate and deliberation approach only works when there is time. Too much deliberation leads to "paralysis by analysis." If there is the proverbial burning platform, the leader must make the final decision promptly.

Additionally, leaders need to push decision-making to all levels of the organization. This approach enables the leader to focus on significant issues and delegate responsibility throughout the organization, a factor that contributes to shared ownership. It also improves productivity because executives need not look over their shoulders; they make decisions for their level and move forward.

Meetings about significant issues are essential. Their usefulness depends upon a willingness to commit to a process as well as respect for others.

CONSIDERATIONS:

- Why would it be important to you to convene your team ahead of a major decision?
- How often do you disagree with the consensus of your team? Why?
- How do you ensure your direct reports make decisions?

How to Find Talent in the Middle of a Crisis

Crisis brings out those who have been overlooked.

Few knew this better than George C. Marshall, who served as Chief of Staff of the US Army during World War II. Marshall had served since graduating from the Virginia Military Institute at the turn of the twentieth century. He served in World War I and was General John "Black Jack" Pershing's aide-de-camp in the following years, then endured the long hiatus between the wars. And endured is the right word; the Army shrunk in size and frankly importance. It was a backwater, and only the hardy persevered.

Between the wars, there was an emphasis on decorum more than competence. Officer balls were a highlight. Training occurred on the campground. There was little emphasis on military exercises that simulated combat conditions. All the while, Marshall kept his eye out for talent (although reports of his "little black book" have been discounted).[72]

Officers who gained Marshall's attention were George Patton, Omar Bradley, Joseph Stilwell, Mark Clark, and Dwight

Eisenhower. When war came, the officers were promoted to the general ranks and proved their mettle in Europe and the Pacific.

Cream rises to the top in hot coffee. Likewise, talent rises to the occasion when the situation grows hot. For this reason, leaders need to keep an eye out for employees who are ready, willing, and able to help.

Identifying the up and comers when all hell is breaking loose is not easy. Executives are typically looking to survive the day, not look forward to succession planning. That's why it is essential to pay attention to what is happening and who is making it happen.

Here are some traits to watch for:

Out of the box thinking. When the world is turned upside down, conventional thinking has failed. You need people who think differently. These are folks who can look at data and see patterns and make predictions that no one else can. They are relational thinkers who construct ideas by joining concepts from different disciplines.

Critical thinking. The ability to recognize that opposites can both be true is essential to strategic leadership. Leaders need to possess the capacity to reason with precision and to propose solutions that address problems.

Introverts. By nature, those who are quiet are observing without calling attention to themselves. You must look beyond "the noise" to determine what quiet people achieve. They are content to let their work speak for itself. (Note: this is not a criticism of extroverts, of whom I am one. It is a reminder that introverts do not call attention to themselves.)

Confidence. When promoting someone, you must ask: does this person inspire followers? Those who inspire have confidence in themselves as well as confidence in people around them. People feel good about following such a leader.

Team ethos. The ability to think of how actions impact others is essential to leadership. A person who knows that leaders accomplish little by themselves but much by working with others creates camaraderie and a sense of community.

Trustworthiness. Do employees look to this individual as a trusted source of information? Such individuals are relied upon for their expertise as well as their reliability. They pull through.

ANOTHER STORY

One final Marshall story, as told by General Omar Bradley, casts further light on an executive's role in the process of promoting. In 1939, after the Nazi invasion of Poland, Marshall had a cadre of young officers around him dutifully executing his ideas. In due course, Marshall gathered the officers together; it was a proud bunch. They felt self-assured and ready. Marshall noted that they had done what he had asked them to do.[73]

No doubt, the group exchanged satisfied smiles with one another. Then Marshall lowered the boom: "You haven't disagreed with a single thing I have done all week." He made it clear that he did not want yes-men; he wanted officers who could think on their own and take action when necessary without being prompted from on high.[74]

Acting in a crisis requires the talents of women and men who can think on their feet in accordance with strategic intent. Waiting to be told what to do never works. Initiative and execution are at a premium.

CONSIDERATIONS:

- What steps will you take to hire people who are different from yourself?
- What can you do to promote people who think differently than you?
- How can you develop the talents of people who are different from yourself?

Patience: Be Quick, but Not Too Quick

"It's not just about speed. It's about patience."

That is what Paddy Payne tells his daughter, Michelle, about how to compete in horse racing in a movie about her life. In 2015, Michelle Payne became the first female jockey to win the Melbourne Cup, Australia's biggest horse race. Her story is told in *Ride Like a Girl*, and while what Mr. Payne said is likely dramatized, it resonates with someone like Michelle who has to overcome adversity. First is her gender—female jockeys are not welcome with open arms—and second, a series of injuries—the hazards of the trade.[75]

"You're all bunched in, you can't breathe, you think it's all done, then the horses all start fatiguing at the different times," explains Paddy to his daughter. "And suddenly a gap opens. And that's God talking to you. And you'd better listen to God, because he will close that gap quicker than you can say your mother's name."

Good advice for a jockey, yes, but it may have resonance when dealing with significant change. Patience prepares the mind for the opportunity. If the "gap" we face had occurred earlier in our lives, we might not have noticed, and we likely would not have been ready.

Power to persevere

There's another line in the film that resonates. "A horse gallops with his lungs, he perseveres with his heart, and he wins with his character," says Paddy. While he is referring to equines, who compete on four legs, the same analogy may apply to those of us who get around on two legs.

Our lungs provide our capacity to learn, and we breathe in as much as we can. Our hearts point us in the right direction and give us the gumption to get up and go. And finally, it is our character that will differentiate us from others. Those who lead with character are those who will lead others to victory.

You can make the argument that patience is what underscores these attributes. Having patience gives us the space to learn and enables the heart to direct and our character to rise to the fore.

Patience for leaders may be more difficult because, by nature, leadership includes the bias for action. Leaders are those who like to be in the fray; by nature, they do not hang back. They plunge in. Therein lies the need for patience. If you act too quickly, without enough forethought, things can go awry quickly. Hanging back, considering your options, and retesting your assumptions gives you the ability to think through your options so that when you do act, you do so more preparedly. Furthermore, waiting provides the leader with the opportunity to prepare his team to seize the chance when it arises.

Speed to the chase, but wait for the opportunity.

CONSIDERATIONS:

- What opportunities lie ahead? List them.
- Should you pursue your opportunities now, or wait? Explain.

Make This Your "Finest Hour"

On the night that Winston Churchill became Prime Minister in May 1940, he confided to his diary that he felt that his entire life had been nothing but preparation for this moment. It was not an exaggeration. Churchill had wanted to be Prime Minister since boyhood. Yet, despite his exemplary military record (five wars on four continents), he was considered by many as a "bounder," someone not to be trusted—until he was the only one left to be Prime Minister.[76]

Britain, at that time, was weeks away from being the only country to stand against Hitler and his armies sweeping across Europe. A non-aggression pact still bound the Soviet Union to Germany, and the United States had yet to enter the war. In a speech before the House of Commons, Churchill noted, "The Battle of France is over....the Battle of Britain is about to begin.... Let us, therefore, brace ourselves to our duties, and so bear ourselves that, if the British Empire and its Commonwealth last for a thousand years, men will still say, 'This was their finest hour.'"[77]

MOVING FORWARD

In times of crisis, people involved in the thick of the action, as exhausted as they may be, want to be involved as long as possible because they feel they owe it to their colleagues.

Soldiers know this feeling: unit cohesion. They want to be there for their brothers and sisters.

Such was the case during the beginning of the Covid-19 pandemic. Dr. Sanjay Saint, the Chief of Medicine at the VA Ann Arbor and the George Dock Professor of Internal Medicine at the University of Michigan, understands. "The volunteerism and openness to change have been incredible. We have been able to cut the red tape and bureaucratic delays in a manner I thought impossible before the pandemic," Dr. Saint said in an interview with the British Medical Journal.[78]

"This pandemic is perhaps the most potent cathartic I have seen to get people to move forward with alacrity," said Dr. Saint. "It has taken less time for us to stand up three new inpatient medical teams than it usually takes to hang a picture in one of the faculty member's offices. I hope this will continue long after the pandemic."[79]

Everyone in a management position today has the opportunity to make this effort against the coronavirus and its impact on their "finest hour." Typically, comparing war to civilian life falls short, but for those on the front lines of Covid-19, lives are at stake. Our health—and that of our employees and loved ones—is at risk, too.

Leaders must lead in the moment, regardless of how much they prepare in advance. If you can indulge in a thought experiment, imagine one year hence. How do you want your efforts to be judged?

"My biggest personal challenge," said Dr. Saint, "is focusing my energy on the things I can control and have responsibility for, rather than dwelling on aspects of this pandemic that are not under my direct control." "When I get frustrated by decisions with which I disagree, or with employees behaving in a non-constructive manner," said Dr. Saint. "I try to remind myself of the following: everyone is doing the best they can. Including me....I also try to provide hope. The end of regular emails should be uplifting but authentically so. Cheerleading is part of the job. It is important to thank people for stepping up."[80]

Assess the situation. Pay attention to what's happening. Be there for others. Doing these things are what it takes to make this your "finest hour."

CONSIDERATIONS:

- What am I doing to make things better for my colleagues?
- What am I doing to keep myself energized?
- What am I learning now that will make me a better leader going forward?

Part 4

HOW TO LEAD WITH GRACE UNDER PRESSURE

© 2020 Ted Goff

"Can we talk about this later?
I have something I have
to get back to."

Grace is a gift without strings.
We pull those strings to make good things happen,
For others and ourselves.
Grace is a gift we give as well as receive.
Grace enables us to act for the common good,
To create community where each of us belongs.

By the Grace of Others

When people who are wronged are the first to forgive, we ask how can they do it? The simple answer is they act with grace. The deeper answer is they act with greater grace. Showing grace in the face of hurt requires courage, the strength to subdue thoughts of revenge. It is human to seek retribution for being wronged. It is superhuman to deny thoughts of hate and act with love. That is what we call grace. Grace empowers us to act with the goodness that resides within us. The more we act with grace, the deeper our ability to show mercy and forgiveness is revealed.

DEFINING GRACE

Gary Burnison, CEO of Korn Ferry, wrote in one of his weekly email missives, "*Grace is a feeling.* It moves us forward—elevating above any circumstance—and always along the high road. It is what makes us inherently human—the better self that shines a light for others."[81]

Grace gives us the strength to persevere. "When crisis strikes, our natural tendency is to think of cause and effect—to try to understand what happened rationally," board advisor David

Dotlich, Ph.D., told Burnison. "But there are other forces at work—and this is where grace comes in. It is the goodness in all of us that comes out in times of pain and suffering."

Grace, a topic I have explored in writing and interviewing for the past few years, gives us space. When bad things happen, our natural tendency is to shrink back momentarily in fear or anger. Grace provides us with the ability to take a pause, to separate ourselves from the immediacy of the moment. If we have been wronged, we want to avenge ourselves. Grace implores us to show mercy. When others cross us, we want to get revenge. Grace asks that we offer forgiveness.

When we are feeling hurt, we may want to isolate ourselves. Grace gives us the courage to ask for help.

GRACE CREATES POSSIBILITIES

Grace is that virtue that permits all other virtues because it is something that touches our hearts as well as our spirits. Grace opens us to empathy, that ability to feel another's pain. In particular, many of us are called to act with compassion, that is, address the suffering as a means of alleviating it when possible.

Grace is granted unconditionally, but it does provoke reciprocity, not through obligation—that is, "I owe you"—but rather through a sharing of goodness. Good was shown to me— we say—so I want to do good for someone else.

There is mystery in grace. Every faith has a measure of it, and as Burnison notes in his essay, the Greeks celebrated it in their mythology with the daughters of Zeus being called the three Graces. More specifically, research by animal behavioralists reveals that the desire to care for one's own is rooted in biology. For that reason, grace in the context of caring may be biological. We humans have an innate desire and ability to care for those closest to us. By extension, that sense of caring can be communal.[82]

Mystery, too, exists in grace because it happens to us, almost out of thin air. It is spiritual. Grace is given without an expectation of return, only an expectation that it will enable some good to occur.

Leaders Think First

Make time to think!

Pause for laughter. *Who are you kidding?* the skeptics cry from the gallery. *Who's got time to think? I am too busy doing. I don't have time to sit and contemplate the world.* In times of change and crisis we feel we do not have to think about anything except what is right in front of us. Yet it is specifically when times are most challenging that leaders need to carve out time to gain perspective.

THINK ACTIVELY

Planning for the future requires thinking. And to be honest, thinking is hard, so let me offer a few ways to be more "thinkful," coining a neologism that should never be used outside of this book.

Author and philosopher, Simon Blackburn, writes in his book, *Think: A Compelling Introduction to Philosophy*, that "To process thoughts well is a matter of being able to avoid confusion, detect ambiguities, keep things in mind one at a time, make reliable arguments, become aware of alternatives, and so on." In short, Blackburn says thinking is our ability to make sense of our world and to engage in it fully with our minds.[83]

Consider the following steps for thinking as a leader.

Make thinking a priority. Make time to consider where you are and where you want to go. Thinking can begin as self-reflection certainly, but from a leadership viewpoint, thinking must be outwardly directed. How do you want to lead? Where do you want to lead? How will we accomplish our goals? How will we overcome adversity? These questions are thought starters. Employ them to engage your thinking process.

Contemplate before you activate. Challenge your assumptions. Easy to say, hard to do. Why? Consider that assumptions emerge from data manipulated by your thinking to become the scaffold for what you do next. Assumptions are primarily theoretical and may not hold up to the rigor of implementation. Nothing wrong with that. It merely means you need to keep thinking.

Integrate thinking into your conversations. Jim Haudan, chairman and cofounder of Root, Inc., (now part of Accenture) uses the term "co-think." It is an endeavor where people in his company think through issues together. Consider it collaborative thinking. As Haudan says, co-thinking "engages the hearts and minds of your people and engages their thinking." Co-thinking accomplishes two things. One, it enables people to collaborate as they think through problems. Two, it sends a signal that "to think" is part of what we do and is therefore essential.[84]

Keep in mind that deep thinking is profound. Answers to your questions do not arise immediately. And if they do, then they may be options, not real solutions. However, if you habituate yourself to thinking, you will put yourself in a mood receptive to ideas that may come when you do not expect them—in the shower, on the Exercycle, or maybe even in your sleep. They would not have occurred if you had not engaged in contemplation. Solutions happen when you apply your thinking process.

WHAT'S NEXT?

Doing all these things will make you alert to what's coming next. Believing that our future will unfold according to plan is wishful thinking. Reality will road test it. We will make changes, and that means we will think all over again.

> *To think is to consider,*
> *To ponder and to wonder,*
> *As well as to challenge.*
> *Thinking requires effort.*
> *Although work is never without effort,*
> *Forethought makes it seem so.*
> *Thinking truly is our work as we ask:*
> *What's been done? Or left undone?*
> *Answers provide our next steps,*
> *Steps that lead us to know more and do more.*

Note: Inspiration for this post comes from a consultant colleague, Jim Kerr, who posed a question about thinking in a recent LinkedIn post.[85]

Two Faces of Courage

In his book, *Profiles in Courage*, John F. Kennedy, then a senator, wrote about three pressures that kept his fellow senators from acting with courage. While Kennedy wrote about what he called "political courage," his insights apply beyond the legislative chambers. Anyone in leadership is prone to such pressures.

THE THREE PRESSURES

"The *first* pressure to be mentioned," wrote Kennedy, "is a form of pressure rarely recognized by the general public. Americans want to be liked – and Senators are no exception." [86] The same applies to many people in positions of authority. It is so much easier to get along with people if they like you. At the same time, if the price of being liked is to forgo hard decisions, the costs can be ruinous. The role of a leader is to make hard choices. Often those choices are not between right and wrong, but rather between two rights (whom to hire or whom to promote) or two "bad" choices (which people to let go).

Kennedy got to the root of political expediency with his next statement about pressure. "It is thinking of the next campaign – the desire to be re-elected – that provides the second pressure on the conscientious Senator."[87] Politicians run for office and want to stay there. Same for executives. Their campaigns for higher office are not in public, but they are long and arduous. They involve doing what it takes to move up the proverbial ladder. They may endure hardships in the form of long hours, time away from family, and even competition from rivals.

"The *third* and most significant source of pressures which discourage political courage in the conscientious Senator or Congressman," Kennedy wrote, "…is the pressure of his constituency, the interest groups, the organized letter writers, the economic blocs and even the average voter."[88] Outside pressure is nothing new to senior executives; no business operates in a vacuum, and it should be responsive to the needs of its stakeholders. At the same time, when what's good for business is bad for the community, or what's good for the community is bad for business, the executives must make the tough calls.

We see this most vividly with issues related to culture and climate change. Good leaders, elected or corporate, find ways to rise above the pressures of the moment. They act with conscience, not always immediately but always in the long run. And when they do, they help their organization do what is right.

PERSONAL COURAGE

The pressures Kennedy revealed—likability, reelection, and external forces—effect a leader's public life. A leader also needs personal courage. "The courage of life is often a less dramatic spectacle than the courage of a final moment," said Kennedy, "but it is no less a magnificent mixture of triumph and tragedy."[89]

Kennedy exerted bravery in wartime when he rescued his crewmates when a Japanese destroyer sunk his PT boat in the South Pacific. He also exercised courage in the face of disease and spinal injuries, conditions that caused him daily pain. Only the one who has endured understands what it takes to face the odds, especially those stacked against you.

Courage is the ability to remain resolute in the face of crisis, show bravery, and persevere in adversity. Doing so with grace under pressure is the mark of leadership, an example that encourages others to follow.

Mercy Me

Bernice King once hated White men.

As the youngest daughter of Martin Luther King Jr., who was assassinated by a White man, this sentiment was understandable, even though she was raised in a family who preached love in the face of hatred. What turned Ms. King, now the head of The King Center in Atlanta, was a simple hug. In the middle of an interview she was giving years ago about the loss of her father, a White man asked if he could give her a hug. King said that the man's hug was so genuine, it broke the sense of hatred she harbored for so long.[90]

Quoting her father, Ms. King, a minister, said, "There's good in the worst of us, and bad in the best of us." Recognizing this truism opens the door to mercy.[91]

Our culture regards mercy as a sign of weakness, and as a result, we end up shoring up the walls around us from which we can lob insults at those with whom we disagree. Social media, so much of it being truly "antisocial," only makes it easier to act viciously and vindictively, and so often, anonymously.

We need mercy. An attribute of grace, mercy enables us to act with kindness in the face of transgression against us. Mercy opens the door to forgiveness because it is rooted in the under-standing that man by nature is flawed—none of us is without fault. Mercy permits us to open our hearts.

EMPLOYING MERCY

Mercy is a virtue, and as such, is not something to be conjured by a recipe. Mercy is a practice of better living for a better us and a better self. Thinking of mercy naturally raises the issue of how to act on it. Here are some suggestions.

Act with respect toward others. View others with an open heart. Give them the benefit of the doubt before drawing conclusions.

Demonstrate compassion. Look to act for the good of others rather than the bad. We all make mistakes. Rather than pounce when you find someone's error, even a big one, remember that the goal is not to shame but to educate them. Better to teach than to ridicule. And the way to educate is by your example.

Resolve to do better the next time. No matter how well-intended we may be, there will be times when we slip into bad habits, lashing out at others, showing them no mercy. Realizing such a fault means you recognize that you, too, need understanding. Apologize to those you have wronged and move forward.

MERCY TO OURSELVES

The author Thomas Merton, a Catholic monk, grounded much of his writing on mercy. "We are not all weak in the same spots, and so we supplement and complete one another, each one making up in himself for the lack in another." [92] In other words, we need to show mercy toward others as a means of understanding ourselves.

The excellent news about mercy is that it is good for us, too. Bernice King, speaking on CNN, iterated this point. Harboring hate is corrosive to the self; it brings us down.[93] Therefore, you cannot truly show mercy to another without exhibiting it toward yourself. Too often, we feel weak and afraid, and rather than admit it, we recoil from it. Better to admit it. Doing so is an act of mercy toward the self.

As we contemplate our "new normal," it is appropriate to shape it with mercy. We have all experienced hardship, even loss. Acknowledging what we had serves as a foundation for what we can regain and do better this time. Let's rebuild with a sense of shared experience as a means of affirming what it means to be human.

Resilience Becomes Stronger with Use

Resilience becomes a watchword when we experience change and crisis.

Writing in the *Wall Street Journal*, Mark Edmundson, an author and professor of English at the University of Virginia, argues that Ralph Waldo Emerson, a giant of poetic letters, is an excellent example of resilience. Emerson, like so many of that era, knew loss up close and personally. His wife died at nineteen, and his eldest son died at age five.[94]

"Life only avails, not the having lived," wrote Emerson in his essay, "Self-Reliance." "Power ceases in the instant of repose, it resides in the moment of transition from a past to a new state, in the shooting of the gulf, in the darting to an aim."[95]

Edmundson himself, channeling Emerson, writes, "Don't make yourself a patient, don't plump the mattress or pickle yourself in Cabernet. Instead, make life more demanding than it has been. Be tougher on yourself; fill your mind with your tasks and go after them, hard. When we're down, we need to get up and fight as best we can—not tomorrow, but now."

There is much to unpack in Emerson's approach. For many, when stricken with grief, the solution is to persevere in life's journey and with life's calling. Some individuals, as we saw during our past year, have done this swimmingly. They have persisted despite tragedy. Others, perhaps the majority, need time to reflect, recharge and yes, mourn.

Perseverance without acknowledgment of suffering may be shortsighted. You may sublimate your emotions, and ultimately yourself with this approach. Doing so may hinder your ability to achieve better results.

COPING WITH LOSS

So many great artists, like Emerson, suffered significant loss. Many great leaders also suffered loss. One in particular was Theodore Roosevelt. Like Emerson, Roosevelt lost his first wife. All of them channeled their feelings, or in our common parlance, "processed" the loss and integrated it into their lives. They emerged stronger for it, and their work attests to that fact.

Resilience is the ability to come back from defeat, to rise again. But as I have learned in this past year, it's also the ability to meet the challenges of a transformed world. The world of January 2020 is no more; our duty is to create a "new normal" that embodies the best of what we had with the best of what we have learned. We will need resilience to do so.

LEARNED RESILIENCE

Over the past year, I have conducted over one hundred interviews with women and men from different walks of life. One of them, Garrett Tennant, a Royal Marine, spoke about how resilience can be learned through training. What special forces do is subject themselves to danger in training and, in the process, learn to adapt by monitoring their reactions and their behaviors so when they are in a combat situation, they know how to act. The fear does not dissipate; it is managed.[96]

Others I interviewed told me how they as business leaders imbued their organizations with resilience. They did it through their example. They put themselves out front, sharing their thoughts about the road ahead. They counseled individuals and sought help themselves when necessary. Such leaders set an example that adversity is real, but so is our ability to manage it.

Nowhere is resilience more critical than in modern healthcare. We saw practitioners—physicians, nurses, aides—stressed to the max when dealing with the overload of Covid-19 patients. A few tragically broke under the weight of the burden. Fortunately, the overwhelming majority did not, but they did not emerge unscathed. It will take years of processing the stress of the pandemic before they are entirely whole.

Resilience is also a physical reaction to stimuli. As my colleague Dr. Sharon Melnick, a clinical psychologist quoted previously, teaches, we need to learn the practice of self-regulation. We cannot always be on; sometimes, we need to be off. Failure to do so leads to burnout.[97]

SHARED RESILIENCE

Resilience need not be a solo enterprise. Some, like Emerson, can muscle through it, but most of us need to decompress, talk to colleagues, and seek professional help to regain our equilibrium. We do heal ourselves, but doing so need not be in isolation.

Resilience, some say, is like a muscle. You can build it up, but if you don't use it, it will atrophy. Never have we had a time when resilience is more necessary, so let's use it.

Whither Wisdom? A Question for Our Times

David Brooks of the *New York Times* wrote a column about the wisdom of self-awareness induced by the examples of others.[98]

James Surowiecki described congregate wisdom in his book, *The Wisdom of Crowds*. Collective wisdom has its virtues as well as its deficits. Know the difference.[99]

Marcus Aurelius, the philosopher emperor, noted the wisdom that comes from paying attention to what's around us, what today we would call "mindfulness."[100]

Self-awareness. Collectives. Daily life. Each has its benefits. The challenge for us is two-fold. One, recognize wisdom. Two, implement its lessons.

RECOGNIZING WISDOM

Recognizing wisdom is a matter of observation. To paraphrase an old pop song, we are looking for learning, as Brooks notes, in all the wrong places.[101] While the "right places" may include traditional places such as schools and the workplace, more specifically, we need to be alert to the in-between occasions. Life is seldom tidy and learning often occurs at the edges when we may least expect it: a defeat, an act of compassion, a note of love.

Recognizing wisdom is a matter of choice. It comes from within us. We decide to keep our minds open so that we give it proper attention when we experience a learning moment. Easy to say, certainly, but hard to implement because we are so wrapped up in the bustle of our own lives that we ignore the obvious.

When we were sheltering during the pandemic, public lives were limited; we were closed off from the broader commerce of the world. We stayed in touch via electronic media, but we remained rooted to our same location. That forced isolation created an opportunity—not altogether unwelcome—to observe our surroundings and ourselves.

Now that our forced isolation is over, we must not forget that we continue to be mindful of our personal needs. Make time to breathe. Listen to the air going in and out. Discipline yourself to notice what you have not seen before. Pause for effect, not just for others but for yourself.

IMPLEMENTING WISDOM

Implementing wisdom may be a harder nut to crack for the reason that a good lesson requires change. As the joke goes, change is good, as long as it does not affect us personally. Adopting a new lesson is personal; it's a commitment to think differently, to do differently. Overcoming our shortcomings requires work to form new habits: physical (*diet, exercise, rest*), mental (*modes of thought*), and spiritual (*purposeful reframing*).

ACTING ON WISDOM

How do we act on wisdom?

> *Work hard to understand yourself.*
> *Pay attention.*
> *Attend to what you have observed.*
> *Do not fear your shortcomings.*
> *Use them as your guides to move forward.*
> *Take heart from your failures.*
> *Gain lessons from your mistakes.*
> *Forgive yourself so you can forgive others.*
> *Demonstrate kindness to yourself as a means of*
> *expressing kindness to others.*
> *Practice, practice, practice.*

"A person's worth is measured by the worth of what he values," wrote Marcus Aurelius in *Meditations*.[102] When you value learning and the company of others who share the same value, wisdom will accompany you.

One step, one lesson, at a time.

Finding Strength in Humility

One thing they don't teach in business school is humility.

That was a line I would sometimes drop in my presentations, and it never failed to get a laugh. Everyone, it seemed—regardless of whether they had attended business school or not—knew the kind of self-importance and, yes, arrogance that newly minted graduates might display. Their MBA swagger lasts until they hit their first roadblock at work and it throws them for a loop. That setback may be an early lesson in humility.

ACCEPTANCE OF REALITY

Those who accept reality are demonstrating a sense of humility. That, however, does not mean they are rolling over. Indeed, humble people are highly self-aware individuals. They know their strengths and their shortcomings. To quote Thomas Merton again, "Pride makes us artificial, and humility makes us real."[103]

Yes, humility is a gift of strength. It is the acceptance of one's humanity—frailty and fragility, but also hope and grace.

We know we make mistakes, but we have the grace to forgive ourselves so that we can move forward, not simply for ourselves but also for those who follow our lead.

MAKING A DIFFERENCE

"To lead the people," said Lao Tzu, "walk behind them."[104] Humility inspires people to follow, and when they see you behind them, in support of them, they are more inspired.

A humble leader is content to put others first for two reasons. One, she knows that the real work is done by people who follow a leader's directives. Two, she is content within herself to recognize her strengths. She echoes the words of Martin Luther, "True humility does not know that it is humble. If it did, it would be proud from the contemplation of so fine a virtue."[105]

A friend of mine experienced the benefits of humility firsthand while undergoing surgery to remove a cancerous growth near the side of his nose adjacent to his eye. The removal went fine. But at the time of suturing, the dermatologist asked my friend if he minded her seeking a second opinion on the closing of the wound.

My friend thanked her and told me later that four of her colleagues came to view his wound. What gratified my friend was the humility his surgeon displayed when asking for the counsel of colleagues. She did not fear that my friend or her colleagues would think less of her. She was only interested in the welfare of her patient.

Humility is a virtue, but there is nothing soft or squishy about it. Humility is forged in adversity and gives us the backbone to continue our journey.

Humility is a virtue, no doubt.
But gaining humility requires more than virtue.
Hard work. Sacrifice. Selflessness.
Humility demands a sublimation of ego, but not
of will.
Willpower gives us the strength to step back,
So that others may go forward.
Humility enables us to see the light in others,
Rather than our own reflection.

Dignity at Work

My colleague, Tasha Eurich, Ph.D., author of the book *Insight*, recently tweeted, "Cultivating a culture of dignity is a central responsibility for leaders. As companies being to reimagine the future of work, leaders need to redesign workplaces to be a more positive force for growth, agency, and physical and mental health."[106]

My response is, thank you. Dignity is not a word we use much these days, yet as we consider what's next in the future of work, dignity must be a central concept. Dignity embraces two aspects: respect for the individual and respect for the work they do.

In 1891, Pope Leo XIII put forth the notion of workers' rights and the duties of employers in his papal encyclical, *Rerum Novarum: On Capital and Labor*. It was a recognition by the Church of the dignity of workers to work in safety and receive fair compensation. Dignity is a human right but too often is not considered strong enough in the workplace.[107]

Dr. Eurich defines dignity as a responsibility of leadership. She quantifies dignity in four ways. Let's take them one at a time.

Growth. People come to work to apply their talents and their skills. They seek an opportunity to grow and develop as contributors.

Agency. Employees want a degree of autonomy and the ability to make their own choices in their work. They also want the ability to determine their career path.

Physical health. A healthy workplace is an environment where people feel comfortable and safe to do their best work. They require benefits that will cover them if they become ill or need to care for a loved one.

Mental health. There are two aspects to mental health. The first is an awareness that mental health is on par with physical health. When conditions such as anxiety or depression become clinical issues, they should be treated without stigmatizing the individual. Second, mental health includes psychological safety, the assurance that employees can voice their ideas and not be punished if they disagree with others.

DIGNITY CREATES OPPORTUNITY

Significantly, the principles of diversity, equity, and inclusion also rest upon the notion of dignity. Diversity means bringing people different from ourselves into the workplace. Equity demands equal opportunity as well as equal pay. And inclusion insists upon listening to, learning from, and promoting those individuals. None of this can happen without respect for who people are and what they can do. That's dignity in the workplace.

As employers create hybrid workplaces, keeping the notion of dignity front and center creates a workplace where people want to be. It makes a value system where people both feel they can contribute and want to contribute significantly. Why?

Because they think they belong. Their workplace becomes our workplace. When it occurs, organizations have a greater chance of fulfilling their mission because they are more engaged, productive, and collaborative.

Sacrifice: Lost and Found

We have sacrificed.

That is a mantra that resonates beneath the surface as we contemplate the return to a kind of "new normal."

We could not have achieved this milestone without the sacrifices of our frontline healthcare workers, who daily put themselves in danger to treat the sickest among us. Nor would we be closing out this chapter without the contributions of tens of thousands of researchers who worked long days, weeks, and months to develop the vaccines that provide us with protection.

Sacrifice, too, came in the form of loss: of jobs, of people, and in some cases, of identity. Our pandemic turned our world upside down. No one was left untouched. Now the question is: what next?

DEBATING OUR FUTURE

Yes, we will debate the future of the workplace: virtual, in-person, or hybrid. But there is a more profound question. What will come of the sacrifices we have all made? We will not be turning back the clock. That clock has shattered into a million pieces.

For perspective, let's turn back to a sermon delivered in 1925 at Westminster Abbey. Fredric Lewis Donaldson, a committed cleric who advocated for workers and would one day become the Archdeacon of Westminster Abbey, described the "Seven Social Sins."[108] They are:

> *Wealth without work.*
> *Pleasure without conscience.*
> *Knowledge without character.*
> *Commerce without morality.*
> *Science without humanity.*
> *Worship without sacrifice.*
> *Politics without principle.*

Sadly, nearly a century later, we continue to "sin" in each category, and so it's worth considering now at this moment of inflection, when the hinge of history creaks, how we might make things better.

QUESTIONS TO CONSIDER

What we do next will determine our lives and the lives of those we love, manage, and lead. For leaders, that means understanding what we sacrificed and how we will use those lessons to make us stronger and wiser. Here are three questions to ask.

> **What did I lose?** Of all the things lost, what mattered most?

What did I gain? Despite the loss, how did this experience make you stronger?

What will I do differently? Going forward, what will you do differently?

These questions are thought-starters to help you put into context the lessons of this past year plus. You will consider other questions. Jot down your answers. Share them with your friends and colleagues. Discuss your conclusions and invite debate. Doing so will enable you to frame the experience so that you can understand it better.

LESSONS LEARNED

Most importantly, what did you learn about yourself?

First and foremost, you survived. That may be the greatest lesson of all. You demonstrated resilience, the ability to bend but not break and even come out better for it, transformed and ready to meet new opportunities.

In his novel, *The Five People You Meet in Heaven*, Mitch Albom writes, "Sacrifice is a part of life. It's supposed to be. It's not something to regret. It's something to aspire to." Now let's get to work, taking the sacrifices we have made and using them to create the world we want.[109]

Aim Low and Be Happier

Keep your expectations low.

That's the "advice" a friend of mine and fellow golfer once received from a golf pro he had hired for lessons. That line has been the source of much teasing amongst us fellow golfers. "How cruel" and "How low," we say as we laugh, knowing in our hearts that the advice applies to us hackers as much as it does to our friends.

On the surface, the comment is cutting. I mean, you pay for a guy to help you improve your game, and after watching you take a few swings, he insults you. Oooh, that hurts your pocketbook and your ego!

Viewed from a different perspective, the advice is precious. I recall reading that comedian Don Rickles, the king of insult comedy, learned to enjoy golf when he realized he was lousy at it and likely would always be lousy. And so, he began to enjoy the game for what it was: a game played with friends.

As a "high handicap golfer" (the correct term these days is "recreational golfer"), I take solace in Mr. Rickles' perspective. Whenever I struggle on the course, which is most of the time, I remind myself that golf is fun. It's a game I do enjoy, despite my high scores. It is a game that keeps you humble. Whenever I hear the pros talk about being good one day and not the next, I shake my head. My golf prowess waxes and wanes from shot to shot.

Golf teaches humility. As my friend Stew says, "What the golf gods giveth, the golf gods taketh." (Pretty sure that passage is in the King James Bible somewhere.) We usually invoke this "scripture" when one of us scores a double bogey after a previous birdie. Humility is essential to golf, and I daresay, life itself.

A MORE POSITIVE VIEW

So, "keep your expectations low" is less a warning than a gift of enlightenment. When you keep your expectations low, you will be surprised at what you can accomplish. The sentiment is not about trying harder; it focuses on what you can do rather than what you cannot do. This advice is not permission to slack off; instead, it's a suggestion to throttle down your ambition. Ambition is necessary to achievement; without the will and the drive to succeed, you are adrift. Conversely, when personal industry is coupled with purpose, great things can occur.

Or not.

Relentless pursuit of what is not attainable is fruitless. Perfection in golf is impossible; only a relative handful, no more than a few hundred worldwide, have the opportunity to compete for serious money and recognition. The rest of us play the game for recreation. Such play may doom us to obscurity golf-wise, but not in our own lives.

Being realistic about what you can do is a demonstration of self-awareness. Tasha Eurich, Ph.D., whom I quoted previously, proves that self-awareness is often elusive in her research. Only a fraction of us—under 20 percent—are genuinely self-aware.

So, when we hear, "keep your expectations low," and accept it, we are acknowledging our limitations.[110]

LIVE WITHIN YOUR AIMS

Such a perception is no excuse for not pursuing our goals with full vigor and total commitment. Instead, it is merely an acknowledgment that we can only achieve so much, and we accept it. Acceptance, in psychological terms, is the first step toward realizing limitations. And in a world where we are bombarded by messages that urge us to aim high, higher, and highest, this self-acknowledgment is a refreshing antidote.

So yes, keep your expectations low and your pursuit of satisfaction high.

Self-Care: Find Your "Fire Escape"

When Ocean Vuong learned that his uncle had died, he took a long walk through the streets of New York City. His uncle, who died by suicide, had only been three years older than Vuong; the two had been close. As Vuong walked, he noticed something, which he explained in an interview with Krista Tippet, host of NPR's *On Being*.[111]

"I kept seeing these fire escapes. And I said, what happens if we had that? What is the linguistic existence of a fire escape, that we can give ourselves permission to say, 'Are you really OK? I know we're talking, but, you want to step out on the fire escape, and you can tell me the truth?'"

Vuong, an author, poet, and MacArthur fellow, relates this concept to hiding our sense of vulnerability. That is, if you are feeling low or depressed, you hide it rather than reveal it. "I think we've built shame into vulnerability, and we've sealed it off in our culture—'Not at the table. Not at the dinner table. Don't say this here…This is not cocktail conversation.'" Vuong adds, "We police access to ourselves. And the great loss is that we can move through our whole lives, picking up phones and talking to our most beloveds, and yet, still not know who they are. Our 'how are you' has failed us. And we have to find something else."

Vuong, who immigrated from Vietnam as a child, is touching on a very private topic. Marshall Goldsmith, the world's leading executive coach and bestselling author, speaks of the concept of being on stage, that is, always being upbeat. It is true for coaches with their clients as well as for executives being coached. We know how to put up a good front. As businesspeople, this is fine; it is standard practice among professionals.

ISOLATION

At the same time, if we keep our vulnerability bottled inside and tell no one, we induce isolation. We cut ourselves off from sources of comfort, solace, and counsel. We gradually withdraw into a kind of shelter of our own making. We may trick ourselves into believing we are protecting ourselves, when in reality, we may be imprisoning our true selves.

My colleague Terry Jackson Ph.D., a change management consultant and executive coach, likes to say that we all need hope. Hope is foundational to our ability to look beyond our present circumstances. Without hope, there is only darkness. With hope, there can still be light, even if it may not be as bright as we would like it. If we shelter our inner selves from others too much, we also rob ourselves of finding hope, the kind that comes from knowing that we are not alone.[112]

It is not easy to reveal one's vulnerabilities. That's why you need a "fire escape." For Vuong, a writer, the fire escape is a linguist metaphor for "being offstage." What is required is trust and bravery. You need to trust the person with whom you share your story. And you need to be brave about what you will share.

BE OF SERVICE

This sharing is an opportunity for others to serve us. As Terry Jackson says, service is our true purpose. While we think of helping others, we can expect the same from others. Give them a chance to serve us. In time we can do the same. Service enables us to fulfill the needs of others and at the same time fulfill our purpose.

And so, we must find our fire escapes, a place to be ourselves, openly, honestly, and hopefully.

If This Is the Worst That Happens...

One day, right before the Fourth of July weekend, the ice maker in our refrigerator died. The weather was hot, and the gin and tonics were ill-suited to warmth.

Later that evening, I quipped on Twitter, asking if anyone had seen that kid Red Grange delivering ice lately. Of course, football fans will know that this was how the great running back of the University of Illinois and later the Chicago Bears kept himself in shape nearly a century ago, delivering great blocks of ice to houses in his hometown.

Days later I called a repair service, noting lightheartedly that not having an icemaker was hardly a big deal. The service rep lowered her voice, saying that I would be surprised at how many people regard having a broken icemaker as a catastrophe. "If not having an icemaker is the worst thing to happens to me this year," I quipped, "then it will be a good year." The service rep laughed in agreement.

Too often, we get distracted, annoyed even, when little things don't go our way. It's easy to become frustrated, and in doing so, we forget just how fortunate we are. A flight delay. A missed dinner. A dying appliance. These annoy us, but in the grand scheme of life, they are trivial. In years to come, such inconveniences are not likely to be remembered.

GAIN PERSPECTIVE

We must put life into perspective. That's easy to say, but our irritation blinds us to reality. We endured more than two years of disappointment and delusion—as well as exclusion and isolation. But we came back slowly to a different form of life—not the same, but different. In some ways, it is richer because of what we have experienced.

We have been tested, and we have survived. Not everyone did. More than a million Americans died. Those are tragedies. They are benchmarks of actual loss. Annoyances come and go. Losses live as scars in our memories.

A NOVEL LESSON

The novelist J. R. R. Tolkien wrote in *The Hobbit*, "So comes snow after fire, and even dragons have their endings." For him, this statement was true. Tolkien was a young officer in what his generation of Britons called The Great War. He fought at the Battle of the Somme. After the war, Tolkien returned and taught medieval literature at Oxford. He also raised a family and told his sons stories that would become great novels of fantasy in time. Fires and dragons do die out, leaving in their wake the possibility of renewal.[113]

> *So, take a deep breath.*
> *Exhale slowly.*
> *Remind yourself of your blessings.*

Take another deep breath.
Exhale slowly.
Smile in gratitude.

POSTSCRIPT

The repair person finally arrived. With a quick look inside the fridge, he shook his head knowingly. The icemaker was genuinely dead. Good news, a replacement would cost only sixty dollars, plus another service fee, of course. So, again, if this is the worst thing to happen to me this year, sign me up now.

Doughnuts Make Me Happy (but Not Joyful)

Joy, Joy, Joy.

There is a doughnut shop not too far from my house. While I wish I had never found it, every time I enter it, I smile. The doughnuts they make are the classic yeast rising doughnuts that are light as air and crusted in a light glaze. Biting into them brings back memories of the doughnut shop I visited when I was a boy on the way home from school.

I feel happy. What I don't feel is joy.

This is not a criticism of doughnuts. Instead, eating doughnuts is a reminder that happiness is ephemeral. It comes and it goes. Happiness is good. Enjoy it, but do not embrace it. (My waistline is a testament to the fact that I should never fully embrace doughnuts.)

What we seek in life is not happiness per se, but joy. Joy is the feeling of goodness (okay, happiness) that we feel when we are at our best. Joy emerges from the pleasure we take in doing what we like to do and are good at. For example, we can excel at a sport and take joy from it. But taking a longer view, joy comes from the enrichment we feel at pursuing a task, a job, or a career that gives us pride.

AFFIRMATION

Deep joy comes from the pursuit of doing something that affirms our capacity to do better. The greatest joy comes from helping others, giving of ourselves to make the life of another better, if only for a short time. How we do this becomes the measure of how we relate to others.

The joy that sustains us is the joy that comes from giving. It may come from giving ourselves to our work by committing our energies to something greater than ourselves. And it is in the giving that joy reaches its deepest richness. Joy comes from the love we express and the love we receive in return.

As we celebrate the notion of joy, it is important to frame it properly. The playwright and poet William Butler Yeats once said, "Being Irish, he had an abiding sense of tragedy, which sustained him through temporary periods of joy." This quip may perhaps be a truism of Celtic folks whose tradition is shaped by dark forces beyond their control. Joy sustains us in hard times, even when we have little to be happy about.[114]

Life is not all joy, nor should it be, but if we focus on the enrichment part of joy, we will find a source that nurtures our spirit, the way a natural spring waters the ground around it.

NOT TAKEN FOR GRANTED

Joy is never a given. We must work at it, and in the working, we find that we encounter our true selves. The Buddhist philosopher Thich Nhat Hanh wrote, "Sometimes your joy is the source of your smile, but sometimes your smile can be the source of your joy." Inherent joy indicates that you have found a level of enrichment. At the same time, recognize that joy will give you happiness.[115]

> *Joy is not a destination.*
> *It is more a journey.*
> *It is not one of pure happiness,*
> *But more of a struggle.*
> *Yet, in the pushing-and-pulling, we find our true*
> *selves—*
> *Open, Ready, Able—*
> *To help others,*
> *And in doing so,*
> *Ourselves.*

Three Ways to Connect Better with Others

Simplicity is often regarded as the "Holy Grail" within design circles. Striving to ensure that form follows function is a mantra that, while stated, is not always practiced. Too often, a project that begins with the simplest of intentions ends up hopelessly complex. Camels—so the joke goes—were designed by a committee.

No less of a challenge is the desire for simplicity in human relations. Yet, since all of us are different, and the permutations among us seem infinite, striving for simplicity may be a fool's errand…or not. While one size does not fit all, those in charge of getting things done can make simplicity their mantra.

How? By the way they behave. Here is where the desire for human connection makes the most sense. We all, or most of us, want to be connected to others. We seek to be understood, appreciated, and loved. That is where simplicity enters in three ways: head, heart, and spirit. Let's take them one at a time.

Head is rationality. Leading with our minds leads us to consider what others want. It means we must deliver conditions for them to succeed. With such logic, leaders know they must set expectations, communicate them, support the work effort, insist on accountability, and acknowledge the results. Within these steps, accountability is essential. The leader sets the tone and follows through.

Heart is emotionality. Leading with our hearts challenges us to deliver what others want. Knowing what others want is not the same as practicing it. And that's where the heart comes into it. We feel compelled to act, not because we have to, but because we want to. We genuinely desire to see others succeed. It enriches us as much as it does them.

Spirit is transcendent. Leading with the spirit provokes us to meet our aspirations for something better. Within an organizational construct, the leader abides with the goal of ensuring that everyone understands the purpose and how they can fulfill it.

KNOW THYSELF

The leader's responsibilities for simplicity have now been described, but there is something else. First, the leader must understand herself. She knows her purpose and how her purpose complements the whole. Such alignment between the intrinsic and extrinsic purpose may not always be possible. Organizations do not fulfill our every need. We as humans must find our purpose and act on it. Ideally, what we want to do personally can match our work, but we know it doesn't always match. Understanding that dichotomy is essential to self-knowledge.

The defining purpose for ourselves can be a journey. It is often an awakening for some people, a realization that this is what I was born to do. For others, purpose is revealed in their work, acknowledging that I am doing what I should be doing. It is fulfilling.

"Life," said Confucius, "is really simple, but we insist on making it complicated." Yes, it is, but striving for simplicity requires time to discover it and a lifetime to practice it.[116]

Hope Is Not an Excuse for Inaction

Hope is seeing that there is light despite all of the darkness.

—Desmond Tutu

Hope!

It is what everyone wants from their leaders, especially in times of crisis. But, as powerful as the notion of hope is, it must be put into proper perspective.

Let's define hope. It is the desire, the aspiration even, that goodwill prevail. Although human history teaches us otherwise, we want to believe that good will triumph over evil, if only for ourselves.

Some years ago, Gordon R. Sullivan and Michael V. Harper wrote a book about the transformation of the US Army into an all-volunteer force. The name of their book is *Hope Is Not a Method*. Its thesis is that as much as we desire positive change, it requires diligence and hard work to make it happen, especially in the face of adversity. In other words, you don't hope for change; you make change happen.[117]

People become weary of change and crisis. They want the light at the end of the tunnel to be sunlight We hope for positive change, but it will only occur if we plan and do our best to execute our intentions.

Hope is necessary to achieve intentions, as well as to endure the present. There are two ways to look at hope. We hope for a better day by acting with positive intention toward others. We also hope for a better future by linking the need for improvement to achieving our goals.

DEEP ROOTS

Hope is rooted deeply within the human psyche. When there is a loss of hope, people lose their will to continue, so when leaders address hope, they must present it in the following ways.

Be real. During the long years of the second World War, there were hardships and setbacks. Roosevelt never resorted to clichés about a better tomorrow. Instead, he believed that the American people would triumph over fascism, but again and again, he parsed his words, reminding people of the hardships ahead.

Be positive. Leaders must embrace the notion that the glass is half full rather than half empty. With fullness, there is the potential to draw upon collective resources; with emptiness, there is nothing. Leaders need to be upbeat. As CEO of Ford during its turnaround beginning in the first decade of this century, Alan Mulally talked about problems as opportunities. Such opportunities could be solved not by him alone but by the joint efforts of the different functions within Ford.[118]

Be persistent. Change is hard and uncomfortable. And while change initiatives may begin with energy and excitement, they lose their appeal without success. People get tired and want to go back to their old ways, even though such methods do not work, hence the need for change. Leaders need to push and push hard to make certain that people do not become discouraged.

As powerful as hope is, some forces seek to deny it. Malevolence aims to destroy the notion of hope to gain power. Those who draw their power from the weaknesses of others present the idea of false hope. They say, follow me to a better tomorrow. In reality, they are saying, obey me, and I will not spare you my wrath. "Hope is important because it can make the present moment less difficult to bear," wrote Thich Nhat Hanh. "If we believe that tomorrow will be better, we can bear a hardship today."[119]

Doing all of these steps will not ensure a hopeful future, but it will ensure that people know where they are, where they stand, and what they must do to succeed.

> *Hope is the candle in the darkness.*
> *Its flame may burn brightly for a time,*
> *But sometimes, something as small as a puff*
> *Or as frightening as a windstorm.*
> *Can try to extinguish it, but does not.*
>
> *Hope is the candle in the darkness*
> *Seeking light.*

Hip, Hip, Hooray for Friends

Within the sphere of human development, there is frequent chatter about the need for leaders to have personal coaches, boards of advisors, allies, and mentors. Roles played by each add different dimensions to a leader's perspective, both personally and professionally.

But sometimes, as is the wont of professionals, we may overlook something right before our noses: our friends. Maureen Dowd, a columnist for the *New York Times*, explored friendship in a recent column with its genesis in a new book by Gary Ginsberg, *First Friends: The Powerful, Unsung (and Unelected) People Who Shaped Our Presidents.*[120]

Like all senior-most leaders, the president lives in a bubble that serves as both protection and shield. It protects the president from unwanted and unsavory characters, but also shields them from people outside their circle. Bubbles become echo chambers, and that's where friends at the highest levels can leverage their loyalty to speak the truth to provide honest and forthright advice.

DEFINING ONE AS A FRIEND

What is a friend? It is a word bandied about so often that it loses its value. We label acquaintances as friends. We label colleagues as friends. We label social media contacts as friends. They may be one day, but not until there is a "give and take," reciprocity of doing for one another. Friends ask for nothing in return, but we do it because we want to.

To me, a friend is one who is invested in you as a person. She likes and respects you and, very importantly, will make sacrifices for you. Sacrifices come to the fore in times of need. For example, a good friend will help you move into a new place or lend a hand with the occasional household chore. Friends are there for one another, in good times and in bad.

Friends, too, are not blinded by your brilliance, even though you may be. They respect your talents but are not in awe of them, at least to your face. They are not afraid to pipe up if they think you are out of line regarding your relationships with others. Bottom line, they are not afraid to call you a jerk if you are behaving like one.

Friends do have limitations. Because our friends like or even love us, they may not always give us honest feedback for fear of hurting our feelings too deeply. Friends, too, may lack perspective on the issues you are facing, and so cannot be good advisors for all situations. And when conditions provoked by anxiety or depression arise, friends may be sympathetic but not therapeutic. In all of these cases, we need professionals at our side. These can be coaches, mentors, sponsors, and clinicians.

RESPECT YOUR FRIENDS

Friends do play an essential role in our lives, and we need to cherish them. A.A. Milne wrote in *Winnie the Pooh*, "You can't stay in your corner of the Forest waiting for others to come to you. You have to go to them sometimes." Milne means you have to make yourself available to be a friend to others, not to everyone, certainly, but to those worthy of investment.[121]

The heart of friendship is reciprocity. Friendship is both a blessing and a responsibility. Do for them what they do for us. It is a sense of mutuality to the nth degree.

> *Friends are friends when they stand beside and behind us.*
> *They see us as who we are—*
> *Imperfect, yes, but approachable, accessible, and kind.*
> *Friends think the best of us*
> *And want it to be so.*
> *When we fall short, friends remind us of our better selves.*
>
> *Some of us have friends for life,*
> *Others for only a short time.*
> *Friendship is not measured in length of time,*
> *But instead in the depth of commitment.*
>
> *True friends are a presence that make us better.*
> *Friendship is not transactional.*
> *It is transformative.*
> *We are wiser for their presence and their love.*

Handbook for Grace Under Pressure: Leading through Change and Crisis

The principles contained in this book provide insights for how to respond in times of flux. This handbook contains suggestions and tools you can implement now to make yourself more effective in times of change and crisis.

TAKE CARE OF YOUR PEOPLE

What Is Our Situation?

Leaders need to be attuned to what is happening within their organization. They need to identify challenges as well as opportunities. They must also gauge the mood and motives of their people. Taken as a whole we can call this "situational awareness."

The following three questions (adapted from a book I cited earlier, *Hope Is Not a Method*) will help a leader get a feel for the situation and what his/her response to it can and should be.[122]

What is happening? Consider this question as a means of taking inventory of what people are doing and what effect they are having. Are things going well? If so, why? If not, why not?

What is *not* happening? Answering this question requires careful thought. The leader must consider what is missing. That is not so easy to determine. It also requires an assessment of mood and commitment. Are people engaged in what they do? If so, why? If not, why not?

What can I do to influence the outcome? Knowing what is happening prompts the leader to act. Very often, that action will come through the efforts of others. That requires delegating authority and responsibility to others to effect change. Some occasions will call for the leader to do nothing, merely to observe and see how things unfold.

These questions can be asked in real time, as situations are unfolding, or they can be used as a method of reflection, to gain perspective.

***

Asking the Right Leadership Questions

Most leaders like to share information with others, but very often they don't know how to share that information because some information they have is still unformed. That's where a good set of questions comes in. When you ask the right question, you can distill answers that are relevant as well as helpful.

Very often it is necessary to narrow the focus so you can elicit the right information. Before you begin an interview, think of what you want to learn. Is it something specific, or is it a process? Is it a methodology or is it a story? Narrowing the focus will enable the individual to provide the information you are seeking.

Here are some sample questions:

- *How do you communicate the mission?*
- *Tell me about a problem you solved.*
- *How did you enlist the support of others?*
- *How do you handle disagreements among staff?*
- *How do you encourage productivity?*
- *Tell me about a setback you encountered. What did you learn from this experience?*
- *Tell me about a challenge that you could not solve. What did you learn about yourself from this experience?*
- *What do you wish you had known when you assumed your first leadership role?*

The answers to each of these questions may be best told as a story. Encourage storytelling when appropriate.

***

Outcome-Driven Conversation

Conversation is the means by which individuals exchange ideas. For leaders, conversations become avenues of exploration and clarification as well explication and closure.

Conversations about important subjects (such as a business transaction or coaching conversation) need to be considered in advance and planned for. When this occurs, the leader is prepared and can be more fluent in his thoughts and express ideas with clarity and coherence. Here are some questions to help you plan a worthwhile conversation.

What do you want to achieve? Itemize what you want to happen in this conversation. Jot your ideas down.

What will you say? List your talking points. Write specific sentences you want to say. (You may never say it exactly as written, but you will have organized your thoughts.)

What will you do when obstacles occur? What happens if your conversation hits a roadblock? Will you continue speaking or table the topic for another day?

How will you close the meeting? It is always wise to leave the doors to continued conversation open. End on a positive note even if you disagree. The positive note can reflect your desire to have another conversation in the future.

One more note: you can role-play the conversation with a confidant or play it out in your head. This way you will prepare yourself for the ebb and flow of conversation and practice saying what you want to say.

***

TAKE CARE OF YOURSELF

Reducing Stress

Stress is the body's reaction to danger. For early man, danger might have been anything from a predatory animal to a hostile enemy. For us, stress results from multiple sources, both at work and at home. The challenge is to find ways to reduce stress and channel it into energy you can use to become more productive.

Step One:

Identify what is triggering stress. It may be an email from your boss or the sound of a colleague's voice. Whatever the trigger is, you must recognize it.

Step Two:

Deal with the trigger. Rather than react, teach yourself to "stay calm." That is, take a deep breath and focus on breathing from the center of your diaphragm. Focus on your breath.

Step Three:

Remove yourself (temporarily) from what it stressing you. For example, wait a beat before opening the email. Take a deep breath, then open it and read slowly. Instead of responding immediately, take a moment to reflect on what you want to say. Then reply. You might also want to take a walk around the office, or pop outside for a moment to catch a breath of fresh air.

Step Four:

Return to work. Focus on what you can do now. Do not stress about what you are not doing. Focus on what you need to do in the here and now.

Step Five:

Repeat this cycle as necessary.

Note: not all stress is bad. Stress induced by your desire to do your best is a positive. Channel it into your work, not into your emotions.

***

Showing Vulnerability

Vulnerability is a component of authenticity. While authenticity is the "real you," vulnerability is that "you" naked—that is, who you are without artifice. There is nothing standing between you and those you supervise. It is the means by which you put yourself on the level of your employees.

When a leader demonstrates vulnerability, she enables three things to occur: approachability, likeability, and respectability. Let's take each one at a time.

Approachability is how you make yourself available to others. The most effective leaders are those who understand their role is to serve others.

Likeability is what draws people to you. While it is not a leader's job to be liked, it always helps if people regard you fondly. A likeable boss is one people want to follow.

Respectability is essential to leadership. You earn respect by standing up for people when times are tough and when you invite them into the spotlight when things go right. A respected leader is a trusted leader.

So how can you engender vulnerability?

Ask questions that elicit information, not put people on the defensive.

Be curious. You want to know how people think and how you can put their brains to work for the good of the team.

Be humble. You succeed when others do. You may be smart, but you will be acting stupidly if you try to do things all by yourself.

One more thing: **lighten up**. Don't be afraid to make light of your foibles.

A vulnerable leader facilitates the bonds of trust by making herself approachable, likeable, and respectable.

***

PREPARE FOR THE FUTURE NOW

Power Questions

Power is a necessary part of leadership and must be exercised in ways that benefit the organization. Such application of power will indeed benefit the leader, but if application of such power is only to enhance the leader's reputation at the expense of organizational effectiveness, then the dark side of power has trumped the good.[123]

Here are three questions every leader should ask him or herself about the proper use of power.

- **What good can I do with my power?** Power can free executives to push the organization to accomplish great things. It can stimulate the leader to look over the horizon to envision new possibilities and act on such possibilities if it will help the business grow and prosper.

- **What harm can I cause with my power?** Executives kid themselves if they avoid thinking of the dark side of power. Recall examples of executives who have fallen from power when they crossed the line by thinking themselves above scrutiny in matters of business etiquette, fiscal prudence, or even sexual appropriateness.

- **How can I keep it real?** Leaders need to surround themselves with smart people who are not afraid to assert themselves even when it goes contrary to the leader's ideas. Leaders need to be challenged by those they lead.

***

Thinking and Acting Strategically

Combining thoughts with actions frames what you do as a means of aligning with the vision, fulfilling the mission, and living the values of your organization.

- **Adopt the big picture.** Study trends affecting conditions inside and outside your organization.
- **Think critically.** Learn to challenge assumptions and evaluate competing options.
- **Get comfortable with ambiguity.** Learn to embrace change and find ways to channel it to your advantage.

- **Trust your gut.** Make decisions based on what you know but also on what you think might happen.

***

Create Community

Community is the sense of belonging we feel when we work cooperatively and collaboratively for intended results. Being part of a community requires living within the principles of psychological safety. Such principles establish a safe environment for people and teams to learn, cooperate, and collaborate. Community does not demand uniformity; it embraces difference, inclusivity, and equal opportunity.[124]

Determine the purpose of your organization.

- Live the purpose by integrating it into your vision (*becoming*), mission (*doing*), and values (*belonging*).
- Communicate openly and transparently.
- Act with courage in the face of exclusion.
- Be bold in your ideas. Be humble in your demeanor.
- Celebrate results. Share credit widely.
- Live with a spirit of grace. Act with kindness and compassion.

***

Lead with Compassion

Compassion is grace in action.

Communicate with an open mind and act with an open heart.

Operate with a mindset of abundance.

Meet others where they are, not where you'd like them to be.

Put others ahead of yourself.

Act for the good of the team.

Serve others as you would like to be served.

Stay back to see what else can be done for others.

Initiate action on behalf of others.

Open yourself to the goodness around you.

Need help? Seek it. You are not alone.

Self-Assessment: Grace Under Pressure

Grace under pressure is the ability to keep calm and carry on. Leading in crisis requires an ability to remained composed, focused, and engaged when tensions rise.

Answer the following questions on a scale of 1–5 (*with 5 being best and 1 being worst*).

LEADING MYSELF

_____ When tensions rise, I speak more slowly and calmly.

_____ I monitor my team's engagement levels by checking in with them on a regular basis.

_____ I realize that my mood can affect how the team performs, so when I am in a bad mood, I work hard not to take it out on others.

_____ I recognize we are working in stressful times, and I make sure I keep myself on an even keel whenever possible.

_____ I know that fear can be a dominant emotion in times of crisis, and I find ways to address it.

_____ I know that anxiety is a common reaction to uncertainty, and I make it safe for my people to discuss it openly.

_____ I bring outside experts to my team to teach principles of stress-reduction and mindfulness.

_____ I maintain my energy by exercising regularly and eating healthy foods.

_____ I make reflection a practice to gain perspective of where the team is now and where it needs to go.

_____ I make a point of engaging my people in small talk periodically to see how they are doing personally.

_____ I know that mental health can suffer in times of crisis, so I communicate the importance of seeking professional help without shame or stigma.

_____ I understand that clarity resolves ambiguity, but providing clarity during times of flux is not always possible.

_____ Leading my team

_____ I keep my people in the loop about what is happening and what is not happening.

_____ I work hard to separate activity from productivity, e.g., I don't conflate the two.

_____ I believe that inclusiveness enables organizations to bring the best talent to the table.

_____ I challenge my team to hire for diversity, treat everyone equally, and include all in decision-making.

_____ I encourage my people to seek out mentors as well as serve as mentors.

_____ I engage my people by setting clear expectations and communicating them.

_____ I ask questions to learn about what is happening, why it is happening, and how I might support others.

_____ I hold myself accountable for my actions, and I expect the same of my direct reports.

_____ I encourage my people to sponsor/advocate for employees different from themselves.

_____ I believe empathy is something that leaders act upon to make things better when possible.

_____ I seek input from multiple sources before making a major decision.

_____ I listen more than I speak as a means of gauging the mood of my team.

_____ I believe resilience is the ability to "bounce back" from adversity as well as to learn from it.

_____ I believe the values we hold dear today will shape the values that will determine our future.

_____ I may work long hours and send emails at odd hours, but I make sure that my people do not feel they must respond in real time at night or on weekends.

_____ I believe that crisis provokes opportunity, and I readily solicit ideas from my team about how we can perform better.

_____ I believe that when times are tough, talent rises to the top. I keep on the lookout for individuals who are doing good work.

_____ I believe that success begets success and that failure can beget failure, so I ask my people for ideas for turning mistakes into learning opportunities.

Scoring:

You rock	130+
You are on the right path	100–129
You can improve	80–99
Commend yourself for your honesty	<79

OPEN-ENDED QUESTIONS:

- *What must I stop doing to lead with grace under pressure?*
- *What can I do better to engage the hearts and minds of those I lead?*
- *When the crisis has passed, what do I want people to say about the way I led?*

Endnotes

Prologue

1   Stacey Flores Chandler, "JFK & Hemingway: Beyond 'Grace Under Pressure,'" *The JFK Library Archives: An Inside Look, John F. Kennedy Presidential Library and Museum* (July 20, 2018). https://jfk.blogs.archives.gov/2018/07/20/jfk-hemingway/.

2   John Baldoni, *Grace: A Leader's Guide to a Better Us* (Pensacola, FL: Indigo River Publishing, 2019).

3   "Grace under pressure" poem first appeared in *Grace Notes: Leading in an Upside-Down World* (2021).

Part 1: Take Care of Your People

4   Mark Goulston, "GRACE under pressure: John Baldoni with Mark Goulston, M.D." Interview by John Baldoni, August 6, 2021, YouTube, timestamp, https://www.youtube.com/watch?v=t7gmh8TN2rQ

5   The quote about adversity is often attributed to James Lane Allen, a nineteenth and twentieth century American novelist.

6   William Goldman, *The Princess Bride* (New York: Harcourt Brace Jovanovich, 1973).

7   "What the Armed Forces Can Teach Business," *The Economist,* (October 22, 2020). https://www.economist.com/business/2020/10/22/what-the-armed-forces-can-teach-business.

8   Gareth Tennant, "GRACE under pressure: John Baldoni with Gareth Tennant," November 4, 2020, YouTube, 8:12, https://youtu.be/P-WdyfuOg3Y.

9   Gareth Tennant, "GRACE under pressure: John Baldoni with Gareth Tennant," November 4, 2020, YouTube, 8:12, https://youtu.be/P-WdyfuOg3Y.

10 Gareth Tennant, "GRACE under pressure: John Baldoni with Gareth Tennant," November 4, 2020, YouTube, 12:20, https://youtu.be/P-WdyfuOg3Y.

11 Gareth Tennant, "GRACE under pressure: John Baldoni with Gareth Tennant," November 4, 2020, YouTube, 25:18, https://youtu.be/P-WdyfuOg3Y.

12 Author Interview with Rita Gunther McGrath April 2020; Rita Gunther McGrath 2020 *Seeing Around Corners: How to Spot Inflection Points in Business Before They Happen* (New York: Paradigm 2019).

13 Author Interview with Sally Helgesen (April 2020); Sally Helgesen and Marshall Goldsmith *How Women Rise: Break the 12 Habits Holding You Back* (New York: Hachette 2018).

14 Warren Bennis, "The Seven Ages of the Leader," *Harvard Business Review,* (January 2004). https://hbr.org/2004/01/the-seven-ages-of-the-leader.

15 Warren Bennis and Robert J. Thomas, "Crucibles of Leadership," *Harvard Business Review,* (September 2002). https://hbr.org/2002/09/crucibles-of-leadership.

16 Harry M. Kraemer, "Two Principles for Leading Your Organization Through the COVID-19 Crisis," *Kellogg Insight,* (March 19, 2020). https://insight.kellogg.northwestern.edu/article/two-principles-leading-organization-covid-19-crisis.

17 Author interview with Sally Helgesen (April 2020).

18 Text to Volodomyr Zelensky's speech to the U.S.
    Congress, (March 16, 2022). https://qz.com/2142992/
    transcript-of-volodymyr-zelenskyys-speech-to-the-us-congress/.

19 *The Role of a Lifetime* is the title of a biography
    of Ronald Reagan by Lou Cannon.

20 "Ukraine's leader defiant as Kyviv holds firm against
    Russian assaults," Alexander Smith, Courtney Kube and
    Corky Siemaszko MSNBC News (February 26 2022).
    https://www.nbcnews.com/news/world/russia-ukraine-
    conflict-zelenskyy-kyiv-battle-putin-invasion-rcna17796

21 "Ukraine's leader defiant as Kyviv holds firm against
    Russian assaults" Alexander Smith, Courtney Kube and
    Corky Siemaszko MSNBC News (February 26 2022).
    https://www.nbcnews.com/news/world/russia-ukraine-
    conflict-zelenskyy-kyiv-battle-putin-invasion-rcna17796

22 Elie Wiesel Quote from his 1986 Nobel Prize
    Acceptance speech https://www.nobelprize.org/
    prizes/peace/1986/wiesel/acceptance-speech/

23 "Inaugural Address of President John F. Kennedy," (January
    20 1961). https://www.jfklibrary.org/archives/other-resources/
    john-f-kennedy-speeches/inaugural-address-19610120.

24 Author unknown.

25 Mary Frances O'Connor, "Grief: A Brief History of Research
    on How Body, Mind, and Brain Adapt," (November 11 2019).
    https://www.ncbi.nlm.nih.gov/pmc/articles/PMC6844541/.

26 Rabbi Earl Grollman (OKC).

27 Author interview with Carol Kauffman (2020).

28 Tony Alessandra and Michael O'Connor, *The Platinum Rule:
    Discover the Four Basic Business Personalities and How They Can
    Lead You to Success* (New York: Grand Central Publishing 1996).

29 Author interview with Carol Kauffman (2020).

30 Author interview with Carol Kauffman (2020).

31 https://www.ekrfoundation.org/elisabeth-kubler-ross/quotes/.

[32] "GRACE under pressure: John Baldoni with Laura Berland + Evan Harrel," (July 6 2021). https://www.youtube.com/watch?v=crPxjpxcf6c.

[33] "GRACE under pressure: John Baldoni with Laura Berland + Evan Harrel," (July 6 2021). https://www.youtube.com/watch?v=crPxjpxcf6c.

[34] Quote from Mother Teresa.

[35] Author interview with David Fessell, M.D. (2020).

Part 2: Take Care of Yourself

[36] *The Wipers Times,* https://en.wikipedia.org/wiki/The_Wipers_Times.

[37] Quote from John Wooden.

[38] John Dickerson, *The Hardest Job in the World: The American Presidency* (New York: Random House 2020).

[39] Author interview with Sharon Melnick, Ph.D. (2020).

[40] Author interview with Sharon Melnick, Ph.D. (2020).

[41] Sharon Melnick, *Success Under Stress: Powerful Tools for Staying Calm, Confident and Productive When the Pressure Is On* (New York: AMACOM 2012).

[42] Sharon Melnick, *Success Under Stress: Powerful Tools for Staying Calm, Confident and Productive When the Pressure Is On* (New York: AMACOM 2012).

[43] Author interview with Sharon Melnick, Ph.D. (2020).

[44] Sharon Melnick *Success Under Stress: Powerful Tools for Staying Calm, Confident and Productive When the Pressure Is On* (New York: AMACOM 2012).

[45] Author interview with Sharon Melnick, Ph.D. (2020).

[46] Author interview with Sharon Melnick, Ph.D. (2020).

[47] Sharon Melnick, *Success Under Stress: Powerful Tools for Staying Calm, Confident and Productive When the Pressure Is On* (New York: AMACOM 2012).

[48] Institute for Coaching www.ioc.org; Jennifer Eberhard https://web.stanford.edu/~eberhard/about-jennifer-

eberhardt.html; Pragya Agarwal Sway: *Unraveling Unconscious Bias* London: Bloomsbury Sigma (2020).

49   Institute for Coaching www.ioc.org; Jennifer Eberhard https://web.stanford.edu/~eberhard/about-jennifer-eberhardt.html; Pragya Agarwal Sway: *Unraveling Unconscious Bias* London: Bloomsbury Sigma (2020).

50   Quote by Jonathan Swift.

51   Michelle Obama, *Becoming* (New York: Crown 2018).

52   John U. Bacon "Now It's Time for Michigan to Face a Familiar Crisis," https://johnubacon.com/2020/02/now-its-michigans-turn-to-face-a-familiar-crisis/.

53   Franklin Roosevelt "Day of Infamy" speech. https://time.com/4593483/pearl-harbor-franklin-roosevelt-infamy-speech-attack/.

54   Khaled Hosseini, *The Kite Runner* (New York: Riverhead Books 2003).

55   Interview with Michael Tilson Thomas, *Fresh Air* NPR (December 6 2019). https://www.npr.org/2019/12/06/785479448/michael-tilson-thomas-on-the-thrills-and-challenges-of-conducting-an-orchestra.

56   Quote from Stanford Meisner.

57   Barack Obama "How to Make This Moment the Turning Point for Real Change" Medium.com (June 1 2020). https://barackobama.medium.com/how-to-make-this-moment-the-turning-point-for-real-change-9fa209806067.

58   Barack Obama "How to Make This Moment the Turning Point for Real Change" Medium.com (June 2 2020). https://barackobama.medium.com/how-to-make-this-moment-the-turning-point-for-real-change-9fa209806067.

59   Author interview with Ron Carucci (2020).

Part 3: Prepare for the Future

60   Christine Porath and Tony Schwartz "The Power of Meeting Your Employee's Needs," Harvard Business Review (June 30 2014).

https://hbr.org/2014/06/
the-power-of-meeting-your-employees-needs.

61 Christine Porath, *Mastering Community: The Surprising Ways That Coming Together Moves Us from Surviving to Thriving* (New York: Balance 2022).

62 Christine Porath "GRACE under pressure: John Baldoni with Christine Porath," (March 29, 2022). https://youtu.be/k0IcGr6aIe8.

63 Gregory Boyle *The Whole Language: The Power of Extravagant Tenderness* (New York: Avid Reader Press/Simon & Schuster 2021).

64 William Goldman *Adventures in the Screen Trade* (New York: Warner Books 1983). https://www.goodreads.com/quotes/457097-nobody-knows-anything-not-one-person-in-the-entire-motion.

65 Reference to "alphabet agencies" https://www.ushistory.org/us/49e.asp (And in reference to the quote from Franklin Roosevelt).

66 Quote from Marcus Aurelius.

67 Quote from W. Edwards Deming.

68 Quote from Michael Porter.

69 Quote from Francis Bacon.

70 Jon Meacham & Tim McGraw *Songs of America: Patriotism, Protest, and the Songs That Made a Nation* (New York: Random House 2019).

71 Marc K Updegrove *Incomparable Grace: JFK in the Presidency* (New York: Dutton 2022).

72 "Marshall Myths: Marshall's 'Little Black Book,'" (December 11 2015). https://www.marshallfoundation.org/blog/marshall-myths-marshalls-little-black-book/.

73 Forrest C. Pogue *George C. Marshall* (New York Viking Press 1986).

74 Forrest C. Pogue *George C. Marshall* (New York Viking Press 1986).

75 *Ride Like a Girl*, Netflix. https://en.wikipedia.org/wiki/Ride_Like_a_Girl.

76 This paragraph reflects the consensus of multiple biographies of Winston Churchill.

77 "This was their finest hour," (Speech by Winston Churchill). https://en.wikipedia.org/wiki/This_was_their_finest_hour.

78 "10 Minutes with Sanjay Saint, Chief of Medicine, VA, Ann Arbor, MI," *BMJ Leader* Vol. 4 Issue 3. (*British Medical Journal*) https://bmjleader.bmj.com/content/4/3/144.

79 "10 Minutes with Sanjay Saint, Chief of Medicine, VA, Ann Arbor, MI" *BMJ Leader* Vol. 4 Issue 3. (*British Medical Journal*) https://bmjleader.bmj.com/content/4/3/144.

80 "10 Minutes with Sanjay Saint, Chief of Medicine, VA, Ann Arbor, MI" *BMJ Leader* Vol. 4 Issue 3. (*British Medical Journal*) https://bmjleader.bmj.com/content/4/3/144.

Part 4: How to Lead with Grace Under Pressure

81 Gary Burnison, "Our State of Grace," https://www.kornferry.com/insights/special-edition/our-state-of-grace

82 John Baldoni, *Grace: A Leader's Guide to a Better Us* (Pensacola FL: Indigo River Publishing 2019).

83 Simon Blackburn, *Think: A Compelling Introduction to Philosophy* (Oxford, UK: Oxford English Press 1999).

84 Jim Haudan, "GRACE under pressure: John Baldoni with Jim Haudan," (July 14 2020). https://youtu.be/jBYLw3RhwEw.

85 Inspiration from Jim Kerr. https://www.linkedin.com/feed/update/urn:li:activity:6793127943431299072/.

86 Excerpts from Profiles in Courage by John F. Kennedy. https://www.jfklibrary.org/learn/education/profile-in-courage-essay-contest/teacher-information-and-curriculum-ideas/curriculum-appendix-2.

87 Excerpts from Profiles in Courage by John F. Kennedy. https://www.jfklibrary.org/learn/education/profile-in-courage-essay-contest/teacher-information-and-curriculum-ideas/curriculum-appendix-2.

88 Excerpts from Profiles in Courage by John F. Kennedy. https://www.jfklibrary.org/learn/education/profile-in-courage-essay-contest/teacher-information-and-curriculum-ideas/curriculum-appendix-2.

89 Quote from John F Kennedy. https://www.goodreads.com/
    quotes/229170-the-courage-of-life-is-often-a-less-dramatic-spectacle.

90 "Bernice King hated white men," CNN.com (video)
    https://www.cnn.com/videos/us/2021/05/25/bernice-
    king-overcoming-hate-sot-oneworld-vpx.cnn.

91 "Bernice King hated white men," CNN.com (video)
    https://www.cnn.com/videos/us/2021/05/25/bernice-
    king-overcoming-hate-sot-oneworld-vpx.cnn.

92 Quote from Thomas Merton.

93 "Bernice King hated white men," CNN.com (video)
    https://www.cnn.com/videos/us/2021/05/25/bernice-
    king-overcoming-hate-sot-oneworld-vpx.cnn

94 Mark Edmundson, "What Emerson Can Teach Us about Resilience,"
    (*Wall Street Journal* June 18 2021). https://www.wsj.com/articles/
    what-emerson-can-teach-us-about-resilience-11624039701.

95 Mark Edmundson, "What Emerson Can Teach Us about Resilience,"
    (*Wall Street Journal* June 18 2021). https://www.wsj.com/articles/
    what-emerson-can-teach-us-about-resilience-11624039701.

96 Author interviews, "GRACE under pressure," www.johnbaldoni.
    com/LIVE; John Baldoni "Putting Resilience into Your
    Organization," *Smartbrief* (November 2020). https://www.
    smartbrief.com/original/
    2020/11/putting-resilience-your-organization.

97 John Baldoni "Dealing with Stress in a Resilient Way,"
    Smartbrief.com (April 10 2020). https://corp.smartbrief.
    com/original/2020/04/dealing-stress-resilient-way.

98 David Brooks, "Wisdom Isn't What You Think It Is,"
    (*New York Times* April 15 2021). https://www.nytimes.
    com/2021/04/15/opinion/wisdom-attention-listening.html;

99 James Suroweicki, *Wisdom of Crowds: Why the Many Are Smarter
    Than the Few and How Collective Wisdom Shapes Business, Economies,
    Societies and Nations* (New York: Doubleday/Anchor 2004).

100 https://en.wikipedia.org/wiki/Marcus_Aurelius.

[101] Story about the song "Looking for Love in All the Wrong Places." https://www.countrythangdaily.com/looking-for-love-in-all-the-wrong-places/.

[102] https://www.goodreads.com/author/quotes/17212.Marcus_Aurelius?page=3.

[103] Quote from Thomas Merton.

[104] Quote from Lao Tzu.

[105] Quote from Martin Luther.

[106] Tweet from Tasha Eurich, Ph.D. https://twitter.com/tashaeurich/status/1433452244993810441?s=20

[107] "Rerum Novarum" https://en.wikipedia.org/wiki/Rerum_novarum.

[108] Fredrick Lewis Donaldson, "Seven Social Sins." https://www.goodreads.com/quotes/tag/sacrifice.

[109] Mitch Albom, *The Five People You Meet in Heaven* (New York: Hyperion 2003)

[110] Tasha Eurich, Ph.D., *Insight: The Surprise Truth about How Others See Us* (New York: Currency 2017).

[111] Ocean Vuong Interview with Krista Tippet "A Life Worth Our Breath" (April 30 2020). On Being https://onbeing.org/programs/ocean-vuong-a-life-worthy-of-our-breath/; Ocean Vuong first described the "fire escape" metaphor in an essay for Rumpus https://therumpus.net/2014/08/the-weight-of-our-living-on-hope-fire-escapes-and-visible-desperation/.

[112] Author interview with Terence Jackson, Ph.D., (April 2021).

[113] J.R.R. Tolkien, *The Hobbit* (quote).

[114] Quote from W.B. Yeats.

[115] Quote from Thich Nhat Hanh.

[116] Quote from Confucius.

[117] Gordon R. Sullivan and Michael V. Harper, *Hope Is Not a Method* (New York: New York Times Press 1995).

[118] Based upon presentations by and conversations with Alan Mulally.

[119] Quote by Thich Nhat Hanh.

[120] Maureen Dowd, "Friends in High Places" (New York Times July 3 2021). https://www.nytimes.com/2021/07/03/opinion/presidents-friends.html; Gary Ginsberg, *First Friends: The Powerful Unsung, (And Unelected) People Who Shaped our Presidents* (New York: Twelve (Hachette) 2021).

[121] A.A. Milne, *Winnie the Pooh* Quote.

[122] These questions were adapted from *Hope Is Not a Method* by Gordon Sullivan and Michael Harper (New York: *Times Books*, 1996) and used in my first book *Personal Leadership: Taking Care of Your Work Life* (Rochester, MI: *Elsewhere Press* 2000)

[123] Adapted from John Baldoni "Stop Your Power Trip Before It Starts" *Harvard Business Review* October 18, 2010 https://hbr.org/2010/10/stop-your-power-trip-before-it

[124] Amy Edmondson, *The Fearless Organization: Creating Psychological Safety in the Workplace for Learning, Innovation, and Growth* (San Francisco: Wiley & Co 2017).

Acknowledgments

Titles are important to books. They are the flags for the ideas we authors send out to let people know what we have written. Titles also can serve as spines for the book, something that holds it together as well as flexes with the breadth of the ideas we share. Such is the case with this book and for that I owe three friends a debt of gratitude.

When I was speaking about how I give "muscle" to the notion of grace, two friends, Christopher Merlo, an author and veteran marketing communications writer, and CB Bowman, founder and CEO of the Association of Executive Coaches, offered the phrase "grace under pressure." Chester Elton came up with the subtitle, "leading through change and crisis." Doing so enabled me to make the book more practical as well as accessible.

My LinkedIn Live show, *GRACE under pressure*, shares themes with the book, and I am especially grateful to the many guests, all thought leaders and doers who are making our world better. These include Ron Carucci, Tasha Eurich, David Fessell, Sharon Melnick, Mark Goulston, and many more.

My colleagues at 100 Coaches helped me think through the ideas in this book, and for them I am grateful. Thank you to Marshall Goldsmith whose idea this group was, and to Scott Osman and Bill Carrier who helped shape and steer its course.

Special thanks to Jan Zucker, CEO of Digital Media, who produced a course based on the principles of this book. Working with Jan and his team helped me sharpen ideas that were contained in the book.

Steve Carlis and his team at 2MM deserve special mention. Without Steve's wise counsel, and this team's great creativity, this book might not have seen the light of publishing. Thank you, Steve.

My book club friends were a steady source of support. They offered me the friendship I needed to round out my life through our shared interests—golf and making one another laugh. Thank you, Jerry, Dan, Stew, Jim, Rob, Bill, Jim and Ned.

And as ever, I thank my wife, Gail Campanella, for her insights and patience while I struggled to put together yet another book. Love you always.

About the Author

John Baldoni is a globally recognized leadership educator, certified Master Corporate Executive Coach, and author of sixteen books that have been translated into ten languages.

John's thought leadership is reflected in his writing as well as his choice of media: columns, videos and books. John also integrates piano improvisations into his keynotes which he illustrates with his still life photos. John is also the host of LinkedIn Live's *GRACE under pressure* interview series, a platform that has enabled him to interview hundreds of thought leaders and doers.

In 2022, Thinkers 360 named John a Top 10 Thought Leader for both Leadership and Management. Also in 2022, Global Gurus ranked John a Top 20 global leadership expert, a list he has been on since 2007. In 2021, the International Federation of Learning and Development named John a World-Class Mentor and named him to its Hall of Fame. In 2018 Inc. com named John a Top 100 speaker and Trust Across America honored John with its Lifetime Achievement Award for Trust. In 2014 Inc.com listed John as a Top 50 leadership expert.

John is also a member of the renowned 100 Coaches, a group of executive coaches and thought leaders from the worlds of business, academia, and social service.

John established a career as a highly sought-after executive coach, where he has had the privilege of working with senior leaders in virtually every industry from pharmaceutical to real estate, packaged goods to automobiles, and finance to health care.

John has authored more than eight hundred leadership columns for a variety of online publications including *Forbes*, *Harvard Business Review*, and *Inc.com*. John also produced and appears in a video coaching series for SmartBrief, a news channel with over 4 million readers. John is the author and host of two online leadership courses: "Leading through Change & Crisis" and "Leading with Resilience + Grace" for Methods of Leaders/100 Coaches.